BEGINNING THE BIBLE...

JOSEPH O'HANLON

Beginning the Bible...

ST PAULS

ST PAULS
Middlegreen, Slough SL3 6BT, United Kingdom
Moyglare Road, Maynooth, Co. Kildare, Ireland

© Joseph O'Hanlon 1994

Cover and graphics by MaryLou Winters

ISBN 085439 496 6

Printed by The Guernsey Press Co. Ltd, Guernsey, C.I.

ST PAULS is an activity of the priests and brothers of the Society
of St Paul who proclaim the Gospel through the media of social
communication

Contents

I offer this little book to my nephew
David O'Hanlon
on the occasion of his priestly ordination

Preface

For more than two thousand years the Bible has enriched the lives of Jewish and Christian readers. It has provided them with their best stories and introduced them to an array of characters, men and women, who live wherever human imagination stirs. But, more than this, the Bible has nourished the faith of these two great communities of believers and provided them with a way of life, with a pattern of living with their God and with themselves. It has formed their saints and redeemed their sinners. It has given joy and comfort in good times and bad.

The collection of books which make up the Bible was put together over a long period of time and represents the thoughts and feelings of people of far away and long ago. This little book seeks to ease the reader into the library of the Bible, to explain why it is there at all and to make sense of its many parts. Newcomers will find in these pages a simple yet thorough guide which, hopefully, will help those who take up the Bible for the first time to become its lifelong friends.

Author's note: Out of consideration for members of the Jewish faith the abbreviations B.C.E. (= Before the Common Era) and C.E. (= Common Era) are used throughout this book instead of B.C. and A.D.

THE OLD TESTAMENT

The Bible is a library of books. Like every library, it is divided into sections. We might think of a library of two large rooms, *The Old Testament* and *The New Testament*, each divided into lots of sections and shelves.

ROOM A: THE OLD TESTAMENT

The books in this room were written before Jesus was born, indeed, for the most part, many, many years before. For as long as one thousand years before Jesus came into our world, the books which make up the Old Testament were assembled from the traditions of a single people, the tiny Jewish nation. That's the first thing we must grasp about the Old Testament. It is not a collection of books written in any European language, much less written in English. It is a collection of books from a small and very insignificant country in the ancient Middle East. It comes from a people who were almost always overrun by powerful neighbours and who longed for independence and freedom. It comes from a people who spoke and wrote a language very different from ours:

בְּרֵאשִׁית בָּרָא אֱלֹהִים אֵת הַשָּׁמַיִם וְאֵת הָאָרֶץ׃

In the beginning created God the heavens and the earth.

Genesis 1:1

It comes from a predominantly rural people, from a world of camels and asses, sheep and goats, lizards and scorpions, figs and olives, pomegranates and grapes. The books of the Old Testament rise out of the stories of these far distant and strange people. They record some of their great poetry, their laws and customs, their parables, their prophecies. Above all, they record some of their great stories, legends, sagas and parables. More than anything else, the Bible is a book of great stories. Readers must be aware of the different kinds of writings within the pages of these ancient books.

An example will help. The newspaper you read every day is made up of news pages, editorial comment, feature articles, sports news, gossip columns, cartoons and comic strips. The sports page is not written in the same way as the editorial comment and the news pages are not written in the same way as the gossip column. As we get used to a particular newspaper, we become familiar with the different kinds of writing it contains. We learn to discriminate between one kind of writing and another. No one will mistake the sport's page for the editorial page. So it is with the Bible. We find there short stories, poems and prayers, lists of laws, bits of history, proverbs and wise sayings, sermons and songs. We must try to understand *the kind of writing* we meet in each book. Otherwise, we will go astray. Fortunately, the people from whom we inherited the treasures of the Old Testament gave some clues as to what the whole thing is about. This will help us to see the wood before we are called on to view trees.

TANAK

Here is a strange Hebrew word. In fact, it is not a word at all. It is an acronym, that is, an artificial word made up of the first letters of other words (for example, QUANGO = QUasi Autonomous NonGovernmental Organisation or NAAFI = Navy, Army, and Air Force Institutes, an organisation providing canteens and shops for British military personnel at home or oversees). TANAK is the acronym often used by Jewish people to refer to their Bible (what Christians call the Old Testament). The word does not in itself mean anything but, as an acronym, it reveals how the Old Testament is divided. We must imagine our Room A divided into three related but separate sections. This is how it works:

TORAH
a
NEVI'IM
a
KETHUBIM

Three words are thus concealed in the acronym: TORAH, NEVI'IM and KETHUBIM. These are the Hebrew names given to the three sections into which the Jewish people divide their Bible. We will look at each section in turn.

The first five books of the Old Testament make up what is called TORAH. The word comes from a Hebrew verb which means "to direct", "to point the way". It is the word usually used in the Hebrew language (in which the Old Testament was written) to refer to divine instruction or guidance. Often the word is translated as "law" and it is true that the word is used in reference to the many laws we find in the Old Testament (613 of them in the first five books). Another name for the TORAH is PENTATEUCH, an English form of a Greek word. This was the Greek name given to the TORAH which was the first part of the Old Testament to be translated into a foreign language. This translation was made in the city of Alexandria in Egypt sometime between two hundred and eighty and two hundred and thirty years before the time of Jesus. The name PENTATEUCH tells us no more than that the first part of the Jewish Bible was written on five scrolls (pente = five; teuchos = a scroll). It gives us no hint as to the contents of the five scrolls. TORAH is a much more informative word.

TORAH: Who am I?

TORAH tells its Jewish readers who they are. They are a Hebrew people, a people with an individual religion which marks them off from others. They have

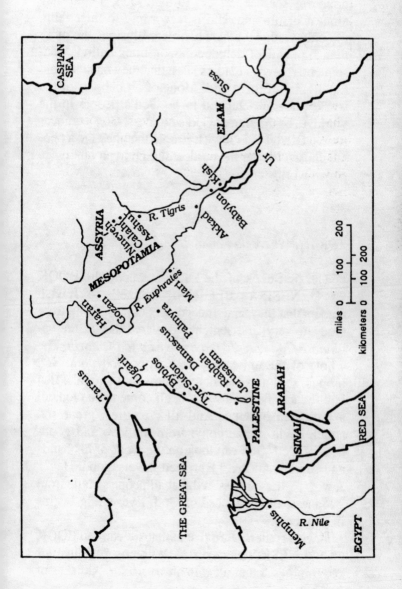

their own ways and customs. Above all, they are bound by the deepest ties to their God, a God they alone worship and who is, according to their faith, the only God. All others are mere illusions, no more than figments of deluded human imagination. Consequently, Jewish readers learn that they must uphold the dignity of their God. Alone of all peoples of the world, they are charged to be God's people in the world, to be the sign of God's holiness, God's uniqueness. TORAH tells Jewish people that they are a people chosen to bear the burden of God in an otherwise pagan world.

TORAH: Where do I come from?

The first book of the Old Testament, the BOOK OF GENESIS or BEGINNINGS, tells its Jewish readers that they, and, indeed, all peoples, come from God. Its very first sentence declares that *In the beginning God created the heavens and the earth.* The whole of the universe comes from God. Suns and moons, seas and mountains, birds and animals, fish and fodder, men and women, all come from God, all are created by God. And all creatures, great and small, begin in and come from the love and goodness of God. God can look on the work of his hands and see that all that he created is very good. Hence Jewish readers are assured that all peoples come from goodness, the goodness of God. Everything begins in goodness.

Jewish readers learn from what we call the BOOK OF GENESIS (a word which means "origins" or "beginnings") that all human beings are capable of great violence and evil and that God is forever engaged in taking corrective action to neutralise the horrors humanity inflicts on itself. So it is that God calls a particular human to begin a people dedicated to righteous living. Jewish readers of the TORAH learn that they come from this man. There are all sons and daughters of Abraham and share in the vocation of Abraham. The story of their great father Abraham and their great mother Sarah is their story. They are bone of their bones, flesh of their flesh. Jewish readers learn from their TORAH that they come from God. But this is not any old God. Their God is the God of Abraham, Isaac and Jacob; their God is the God of Sarah, of Rebecca, of Leah and Rachel. Their God is the God of their fathers and mothers. They come from the vision of their ancestors into the very nature of God. That's how they come to be God's people.

TORAH: Where am I going?

The first answer given to Jewish readers of TORAH is that they are going to Egypt. The second answer is that they are going to *a land flowing with milk and honey*. They are destined to be a wandering people but a wandering people who have a homeland and know where it is. Jewish readers will learn from their TORAH that they are a people forever going home. The land of Israel is their promised land, promised by the God of Abraham, Isaac and Jacob. TORAH recounts the difficulty of getting there. The BOOK OF EXODUS recounts how the might of God must bend to the task of getting his people from Egypt to the promised land. The rest of the Old Testament is concerned, to a considerable extent, with how to hold on to God's little acre.

Behind all this travelling to Egypt, out of Egypt, into the promised land, out of it into exile (a frequent occurrence) and back again, there is a profound lesson for Torah readers. In the muddle of all this movement lies a deeper destiny. Where, says the reader of TORAH, are we going? God replies, *You are going to be free!*

TORAH: How do I live?

Divine instruction, divine guidance, divine directions which point the way are of the essence of TORAH. Its readers learn how they are to live, what they must do in order to be God's people to the world. For TORAH teaches its Jewish readers that they are not given their insights into God, their own land and destiny, without obligation. They must live as God tells them to live. As they journey from Egypt to the holy land, as they wander from one place to another, well illustrated in the BOOK OF NUMBERS, they come to understand that they are called to a way of life. They are called to live in a special way. Jewish readers of the TORAH learn from the BOOK OF LEVITICUS the details of their way of life. They learn from the BOOK OF DEUTERONOMY the purpose of the way of life to which they are called. Its purpose is to create a holy people. TORAH teaches its would-be adherents that the purpose of their creation, the meaning of their journey, the destiny to which they are called may be summed up in one sentence: *I shall be your God and you shall be my people.*

FIVE BOOKS OF TORAH

GENESIS

Name: The Greek word for the first book of the Old Testament comes from the Hebrew original. It means "origin", "beginning". The book opens with the words, *In the beginning God created the heavens and the earth.*

Date: The book purports to cover all human history from creation to the death of Joseph (the one with the dreamcoat!) in Egypt. The stories which make up this huge enterprise were told over many years and put together over a long period. The version which we know probably was not finalised until about five hundred years before the days of Jesus.

Author: Tradition has it that Moses wrote the five books of TORAH. But this is a pious legend. TORAH was put together out of many different traditions over a very long period of time. This is true of the BOOK OF GENESIS and the other four books of TORAH.

Summary: The BOOK OF GENESIS is a book of origins and beginnings. Everything originates with God, the universe, men and women and their children, the birds of the air and the flowers of the field. But there is the beginning of evil and violence, the beginning of murder and death. Original blessings are twisted into sin. New beginnings are required, the beginning of a new people, beginnings with Abraham, Isaac and Jacob, the beginning of knowing God, of loving and serving God. GENESIS is the beginning of a great story, amidst a host of stories. In the beginning and in the end there is God's steadfast love.

EXODUS

Name: The name comes from the Greek language and means "a going out", "a marching out", "a solemn procession". All three meanings can be discerned in the rescue by God of some Hebrew slaves from Egypt.

Date: The date of the events recorded in EXODUS is difficult to determine. Usually, the date of the escape from Egypt is thought to be during the reign of Pharaoh Rameses II (1290-1224 B.C.E.). The date of the final composition of the book cannot be determined with accuracy but it is much later than the time of Moses.

Author: Unknown. The book is based on many ancient traditions but it is impossible to say when or by whom they were assembled together to form one book.

Summary: The BOOK OF EXODUS is about the journey out of slavery in Egypt, initiated by God, to bring his people to the holy Mount Sinai where he makes a solemn agreement (covenant) with them to be their God. There, in God's presence, the people accept the gift of the Ten Commandments, pledging themselves to be a faithful and holy people. The building of a special tent (Tabernacle) as the place of God's presence among his people foreshadows the building of the Temple in Jerusalem many years later.

Name: A Latin word, LEVITICUS comes from the name of one of the sons of Jacob, namely, Levi. He was the ancestor of all priests and their attendants (Levites) who served leading roles in the people's worship of God.

Date: The book presents itself as a record of legislation given by God at Mount Sinai to Moses and passed on by him to the priests concerning their particular role in the life of God's holy people. Thus the book purports to come from the very days of the journey of the Exodus. In fact, the codification of so many laws must have taken a very long period of time.

Author: Like all books of TORAH, the BOOK OF LEVITICUS is credited to Moses but, while no doubt Moses was one of the great legislators for his people, he was long dead by the time all the laws concerning priests and their concerns were assembled in one book.

Summary: The BOOK OF LEVITICUS is a law book. It brings together laws governing sacrifices of all kinds, laws concerning the ordination of priests, laws about clean and unclean practices ("unclean" means "unacceptable to God". Jewish people believe that certain activities and the eating of certain foods make one ritually unclean, that is, unfit to undertake holy duties. This is not a matter of having dirty hands. Ritual uncleanness has to do with fitness for worship). There are laws governing the proper celebration of feast days and the liturgical calendar.

NUMBERS

Name: Twice in this book a census or numbering of the people is taken. Hence its name.

Date: The book purports to be an account of various activities which occurred in the first few years after leaving Egypt, including the conquest of some territory to the east of the Jordan river. However, once again, we must realise that the final compilation of written accounts of such events was made much later.

Author: Again, allegedly Moses but, in truth, the book was compiled much later.

Summary: The BOOK OF NUMBERS recounts various events which are said to have taken place as the people, under the leadership of Moses, made their way through the desert of Sinai and up the eastern side of the Jordan river. It opens with a census of the tribes, then the duties of Levites are spelled out, followed by their various assignments. The incidents concerning water from the rock, manna and quail are told. There is a rebellion and a successful encounter with local kings in the business concerning Balaam and his famous ass. Another census is held and Joshua is appointed successor to Moses.

DEUTERONOMY

Name: In the reign of a certain King Josiah (640-649 B.C.E.), while renovations were being done on the Temple in Jerusalem, a scroll was found which was regarded as a kind of second edition of the law as given by Moses. The scroll was probably an early edition of what we now call the BOOK OF DEUTERONOMY. Its name is derived from Greek and means "the second law".

Date: While the book is projected back into the days of Moses, it comes (almost certainly) in its first format from the days of Josiah and, in the edition which became part of the Old Testament, from the days of the Exile in Babylon (see below).

Author: Again, allegedly Moses. But it seems very likely that the book is an update of ancient legislation and that it was prepared, in part, for the reform of religion initiated by King Josiah. Further additions were made during the Exile. What is important to note is that this book was certainly written by priests and its content reflects matters of interest to priests. Furthermore, it is very possible that the kind of people who put this book together were responsible for the final editing of all the five books which make up TORAH. A careful reading of TORAH will uncover priestly fingerprints all over the place.

Summary: In the BOOK OF DEUTERONOMY there are three great sermons of Moses encouraging the people to remain faithful to their God and to the way of life to which they have been called. There are further lists of laws, concerning justice, the care of the poor and of strangers. There are laws concerning proper sexual relations and divorce. Joshua is commissioned to lead the people into the promised land. At the end of the book, they are poised to enter but Moses is not permitted a final triumph. He dies in

Jordan and is buried there, where we do not know. All we are told is that God buried Moses. The book ends as the people are poised to press forward into *the land flowing with milk and honey*.

A SUMMARY OF TORAH

Jewish readers of TORAH find an excellent summary of who they are, where they came from and what they were destined to be in the BOOK OF DEUTERONOMY. This is how it tells the long story in a few words:

A wandering Aramean [= Hebrew = Jew] was my father; and he went down into Egypt and sojourned there, few in number; and there he became a nation, great, mighty and populous. And the Egyptians treated us harshly, and afflicted us, and laid upon us hard bondage. Then we cried to the Lord the God of our Fathers, and the LORD heard our voice, and saw our affliction, our toil, and our oppression; and the LORD brought us out of Egypt with a mighty hand and an outstretched arm, with great terror, with signs and wonders; and he brought us into this place and gave us this land, a land flowing with milk and honey.

Deuteronomy 26:5-9

The Jewish reader needed to know how to live as befits one of a chosen people. This, too, was to be found in TORAH:

Hear, O Israel: The LORD our God is one LORD; and you shall love the LORD your God with all your

30

heart, and with all your soul, and with all your might.

Deuteronomy 6:4-5

And

You shall love your neighbour as yourself.

Leviticus 19:18

In these three quotations we have perfectly sum-marised what it means to be a religious Jew. We have, too, of course, a perfect summary of holy TORAH.

The second word concealed in the acronym TANAK is NEVI'IM. The word means PROPHETS and refers to the second section of books which make up the Old Testament. Christian Bibles usually follow the TORAH or the PENTATEUCH with a section entitled THE HISTORICAL BOOKS but this is misleading for there are no historical books in the Old or the New Testament, that is to say, no book of the Bible sets out to teach a history lesson. But all set out to impart religious instruction and it is this which is highlighted by entitling the second section NEVI'IM or THE PROPHETS.

THE PROPHETS: What is a prophet?

Most religions have their shamans, witch-doctors, inspired individuals or prophets. They function as protectors of the faith. Such people speak and act on behalf of the god or gods of the people. The speech of the prophets in the Old Testament is founded on one phrase: *Thus says the* LORD. Prophets dare to maintain that they can discern the mind of God and speak on his behalf. Prophets look at the world and its doings and give the God's-eye point of view. Many of the books in the NEVI'IM section are concerned with the doings of kings and queens but they are not concerned with the political, economic or social programmes of such powerful people. They are concerned to evaluate their activities from a religious point of view. How well does such and such a king or queen live and promote the TORAH? How well do the king's subjects live up to the high demands of TORAH?

Prophets saw themselves as the guardians of TORAH. Consequently, they did not hesitate to berate kings for their short-comings and to admonish them on the necessity of mending their ways. Read how the prophet Nathan takes King David to task for his adultery with Bathsheba and note the consequences, both bad and good (2 Samuel 11:2–12:25). Prophets counselled kings on matters religious. It was a woman prophet, Huldah, who advised King Josiah on the importance of the scroll found in the Temple, thus providing a programme for the king's religious reforms (2 Kings 22). Indeed, great prophets such as Elijah, Isaiah and Jeremiah could turn their attention to the whole nation and warn it of the consequences of infidelity.

PROPHETS: Why are they needed?

Prophets were not kill-joys and gloom merchants. True, they speak of gloomy matters. But this is so because they champion the poor against the rich, the powerless against the powerful, the downtrodden against the tyrant. They articulate the pain of the people and go into the public domain, the court of the king or the gates of the city, and weep for the people. Their weeping and angry words are the weapons of the weak against the swords of the strong. Righteousness and justice are always on the agenda of the prophets because these are the values championed by TO-RAH, the very values promoted by God himself.

But prophets do not merely lament present woes. They provide the materials out of which a new future may be built. They inspire people to imagine a new, an alternative future and, accordingly, they empower them to bring about change. To the unimaginative upholder or victim of the *status quo* who maintains that things will always be the same, the prophets provide a vision of new possibilities and an agenda to turn the vision into a new world. Can swords be turned into ploughs? For God's prophet there is only one answer: *Yes!*

EIGHTEEN BOOKS OF PROPHETS

First Shelf : The Early Prophets

JOSHUA

Name: Named after Joshua, its hero.

Date: The book reads like an eye-witness account of a military campaign but it was written long after the events it recounts, probably after 586 B.C.E.

Author: Traditionally assigned to Joshua, the book was written by an unknown hand long after its hero's death.

Summary: An account of the three military campaigns which turned the land of Canaan into Israel, to which is added a renewal of the people's dedication to God. The book is a prophetical witness to God's determination to give the land to his people, a book owing more to hope than to history.

JUDGES

Name: So-called after the fifteen judges whose stories as temporary leaders of the people it relates.

Date: The incidents narrated occurred between the death of Joshua and the rise of the monarchy.

Author: The prophet Samuel (see below) may have had a hand in fashioning traditions behind this book but it was written much later.

Summary: A series of attacks on the people show that the conquest of the land was more protracted than the BOOK OF JOSHUA would have us believe. Local leaders (judges) were called to be "national" leaders and to protect hard-won footholds in the land. Faithlessness leads to defeat, repentance guarantees victory. The stories of Deborah and Samson are particularly memorable.

1 and 2 SAMUEL

Name: Called after the prophet who dominates much of its pages.

Date: The book records events from the days of the judges to the death of King Saul about 1000

B.C.E. but was written, for the most part, long afterwards.

Author: Unknown but the writer may have had some court records to work with.

Summary: These two scrolls describe the rise of kingship among God's people and the part played by Samuel in that event. The career of the first king, King Saul, and the beginning of that of King David are recorded. Particular attention is paid to the friendship of David and Jonathan.

1 and 2 KINGS

Name: So-called because they present the story of the kings of Israel and Judah down to the destruction of Jerusalem and the sending into exile (586 B.C.E.).

Date: These books may have been written during the exile (586-538 B.C.E.).

Author: Unknown. But it is more than likely that the author had access to court records, a sort of Annals of the King compiled by court historians.

Summary: The scrolls present the reign of Solomon and of all subsequent kings from a religious stance. If they upheld TORAH, as Hezekiah and Josiah did, praise is given. If not, they are condemned, whatever their economic or polital successes. The careers of the prophets Elijah and Elisha are highlighted.

Second Shelf: Three Major Prophets

The ministry of Amos (see below) ushers in the golden age of prophecy in Israel. Amos preached in Bethel around 750 B.C.E. and the prophetic voice grew silent shortly after the return from exile which began in 538 B.C.E. The three giants of Old Testament prophecy are Isaiah, Jeremiah and Ezekiel. They speak with passion and conviction, they paint with vivid and daring colours, they see a glorious future born out of the pain of the world. They do not hesitate to chronicle human failure and to lambast godlessness. But each seeks to forge for humanity a destiny which is none other than the heart of God himself. Hope, not despair, is the keynote of great prophets.

ISAIAH

Name: Named after the prophet whose words and ministry and that of his followers the book recalls.

Date: The first part of the book (chapters 1 – 39) covers the period 750-700 B.C.E. and particularly the reigns of King Ahaz and King Hezekiah of Judah. The second part (chapters 40-55) would appear to come from about two centuries later, perhaps, from the time of the exile in Babylon. The third section reflects conditions prevailing as the exiles returned to Jerusalem (after 538 B.C.E.).

Author: Most of the first part is attributed to Isaiah himself, the second and third parts to unknown disciples of the great prophet.

Summary: The first part deals with the prophet's re-actions to various political manoeuverings of the kings of Judah. Isaiah invariably cautioned keeping out of power politics in the region, advocating trust in God's providence.

The second part reflects very different political cir-cumstances. The people of Judah are in exile in Babylon but there is hope that, as shifts in the inter-national power game take place, the exile will soon end. Hence the book is called "The Book of the Con-solation of Israel".

The third part appears to be a mixture of material from the exile period and afterwards and reflects the note of hope engendered in the second part.

JEREMIAH

Name: The book takes its name from the Jerusalem prophet Jeremiah.

Date: Jeremiah was born about 640 B.C.E. He lived through the hopeful days of the religious reforms of King Josiah but witnessed the destruction of Jerusa-lem and its Temple by Chaldean empire. Most of the inhabitants were exiled (586 B.C.E.). Some years later, Jeremiah died in exile in Egypt.

Author: For the most part, Jeremiah. Jeremiah pro-vides more autobiographical material than any of his fellow prophets.

Summary: The stirring times through which Jeremiah lived form the background for the admonitions, dire warnings and terrible predictions directed against kings, priests and people. Jeremiah portrays the faithlessness of the people and his own doubts and inadequacies. But he is not a prophet of despair. Jeremiah believed that true religion comes from the heart and, throughout the heart-searching in this book, can be discerned a man of passion and compassion, a man who loved his God and his people.

EZEKIEL

Name: The book is named after Ezekiel, a prophet and priest who spent his life in exile in Babylon following the deportations there after 586 B.C.E.

Date: Ezekiel lived and worked among the Jews deported to Babylon and his work reflects the concerns of that community.

Author: The inspiration for the book goes back to the prophet himself but there are good grounds for holding that, in its final form, it was put together by his disciples.

Summary: Ezekiel presents three sections: (1) A diatribe against the faithless people who inhabited Jerusalem before the exile (chapters 4-24); (2) A negative judgement on seven nations singled out because they are guilty of inciting faithless Judah (chapters 25-32); (3) A section offering comfort to those who underwent the siege of Jerusalem and subsequent exile and promising a glorious restoration in the land of Judah (chapters 33-48). Ezekiel is full of strange visions and symbols.

Third Shelf: The Twelve Later Prophets

The Twelve Later or Minor Prophets are not to be regarded as either later than or inferior to the Isaiah, Jeremiah or Ezekiel. Some are earlier and some are equally profound. But all are shorter than the others. Readers should note that the BOOK OF DANIEL is included with the KETHUBIM (THE WRITINGS) in the Jewish Bible.

HOSEA

Name: Named after Hosea, a prophet of Israel, the northern kingdom.

Date: Hosea lived through terrible times. His ministry was during and after the reign of King Jeroboam II, a time of prosperity for the powerful, followed by anarchy.

Author: Hosea.

Summary: Hosea loved his wife deeply but she deserted him for a life in prostitution. He tried repeatedly to win her back. The prophet sees in his personal tragedy an image of God and his beloved but faithless people who have prostituted themselves to false gods. Faithless kings, idolatrous priests, foreign powers – all contribute to the oppression and corruption of a down-trodden, dispirited people. Only God's love will serve.

JOEL

Name: Named after its author, the prophet Joel, a man of Judah.

Date: Joel carried on his ministry in Judah at the time Hosea was preaching in the north.

Author: Joel or a disciple.

Summary: Enemies, like locusts, will plague God's land because of faithlessness. But heartfelt repentance will bring deliverance and all enemy nations will be judged in the Valley of Jehoshaphat (Judgement) and God's people vindicated. A farmer's prophet.

AMOS

Name: Named after the prophet Amos who, though born near Bethlehem, preached in the northern city of Bethel.

Date: Amos, a near contemporary of Hosea, preached during the reign of Jeroboam II, a time when the rich got richer and the poor were hideously exploited.

Author: Much of the book goes back to Amos but there are later additions which cause confusion.

Summary: A prophet of social justice, Amos attacks those who batten off the poor and cheat their way to prosperity. He condemns foreign nations who devour Israel and then rounds on the enemy within. But in the end God will intervene to restore justice for all godly people, Jew and Gentile. A shepherd's prophet.

OBADIAH

Name: Named after the prophet Obadiah, a native of Judah but otherwise obscure.

Date: A difficult book to date as it fits into many moments of history. Probably, it comes from sometime after the fall of Jerusalem in 586 B.C.E. when the Edomites took advantage of their northern neighbour's misfortunes.

Author: Obadiah, though the bones of what he has to say may be found in Jeremiah 49:7-22.

Summary: The prophet condemns neighbouring Edom for taking advantage of Judah's woes. He hopes they will get their comeuppance.

JONAH

Name: Named after its fictional hero, himself named after a Galilean prophet briefly mentioned in 2 Kings 14:25.

Date: Probably, this book comes from shortly after the exiles returned to Jerusalem after 538 B.C.E. and challenges the narrow nationalistic religious views of those who returned.

Author: Unknown but someone with a great sense of humour.

Summary: A fictional prophet disobeys God's instructions to preach in Nineveh, the capital of the hideous empire which destroyed Israel (721 B.C.E.). But God insists that mercy and forgiveness is for everyone – even cows!

MICAH

Name: Named after the Judean prophet Micah.

Date: Micah was a contemporary of Hosea and Isaiah and so a witness to the events which led to the destruction of Israel in 721 B.C.E. But some of his book reflects much later times.

Author: While much of the book may be assigned to Micah, considerable parts of it reflect post-exilic times and must be credited to some who cherished the words of the prophet and added to them.

Summary: For its unjust treatment of the poor, for its insincere worship and venal priests, for its corrupt judges and cheating traders, Judah will suffer the same fate as Samaria (the northern kingdom of Israel). But God acknowledges repentance. Micah 5:2 and 6:8 are most memorable.

NAHUM

Name: Named after the Galilean prophet Nahum.

Date: The book reflects the joy which greeted the news that Nineveh, the capital of hated Assyria, was destroyed. Hence, a date shortly after 612 B.C.E. suggests itself.

Author: Mainly Nahum with some later additions.

Summary: Nahum is a vengeful celebration of an enemy's defeat. News of Nineveh's destruction is called "gospel". Understandable, but not nice.

HABAKKUK

Name: Named after the prophet Habakkuk of whom nothing is known.

Date: The subject matter would appear to suggest that the book emerged soon after the first sack of Jerusalem by the Chaldeans (Babylonians) in 597 B.C.E.

Author: While nothing is known of the author, from his words we can deduce that he was an innovative thinker. He challenges God to justify his policies!

Summary: Is God right to use cruel tyrants to punish his people? Why should evil despots be used by God to create more evil? How can anyone with a sense of justice tolerate this? The answer, *the righteous shall live by his faith* (2:4) has a great future!

ZEPHANIAH

Name: Named after its author the prophet Zephaniah who may well have been the great great grandson of King Hezekiah.

Date: The author says he is writing in the time of King Josiah (640-609 B.C.E.) but the condemnatory tone of the book would suggest that he is writing in the early days of the reign before the religious reforms of that king got underway.

Author: Zephaniah.

Summary: The evils which flourish in Judah and are endemic throughout all the nations will be subject to terrible judgement of *the day of the Lord*. The latter phrase is used by many of the prophets to refer to the time of God's final and definitive intervention to put to rights the sinfulness of humanity.

HAGGAI

Name: Named after the prophet Haggai.

Date: The book comes from the days immediately following the return of the exiles to the ruined Jerusalem after 538 B.C.E. and was written in the autumn of 520 B.C.E.

Author: Haggai probably was one of the first to return from Babylon. The graves of Haggai and Nahum are venerated on the Mount of Olives to this day.

Summary: This little book makes one plea to the returned exiles: please rebuild God's Temple, as a priority. Prosperity will come only when God's house is at the heart of restoration programmes.

ZECHARIAH

Name: Named after the prophet Zechariah, contemporary and near neighbour of Haggai.

Date: Assigned to within two months of Haggai's prophecy and reflecting the same concerns.

Author: The first eight chapters come from Zechariah and the remainder from the days following the take-over of Palestine by Alexander the Great (336-323 B.C.E.) and his Greek cohorts.

Summary: The first part consists of eight visions which foretell the rebuilding of the Temple, the restablishment of the authority of the High Priest (Joshua) and the re-emergence of the kingship (Branch). The second part castigates ancient oppressors (Egypt; Assyria) and the newly arrived Greeks (Javan). Zechariah looks to a time when the yoke will be lifted. Early Christians saw many prophecies of the Messiah in these chapters.

MALACHI

Name: Named after Malachi.

Date: The exiles have returned, the Temple rebuilt, the initial fervour grown cold. A date about a hundred years after the return suggests itself.

Author: Nothing is known of Malachi. Indeed, since the name means "my messenger" (see 3:1), the author may be hiding in anonymity.

Summary: Malachi bemoans the fall away from the fervour of the returned exiles. Once again, priests and peoples have failed to live their faith. He condemns marriages with foreigners and (alone in the Old Testament) divorce. On *the day of the Lord*, the wicked will be destroyed and a new moral order created.

A SUMMARY OF NEVI'IM (THE PROPHETS)

All the books of THE PROPHETS defend God's holy TORAH and castigate those who violate the holy way of life it engenders. The great prophetical voices call king and peasant, priest and prince, to repentance. All are called to convert to a new, God-centred vision of things, not only because this is what TORAH demands, but in order to avoid God's wrath. At the centre of the prophetical plea is a call to justice and righteousness. In TORAH, God has shown us how to live. The prophets call us back to where we ought to be. MICAH provides the perfect summary:

[The LORD] has showed you, O man, what is good;
and what does the LORD require of you
but to do justice, and to love steadfastly,
and to walk humbly with your God?

Micah 6:8

The third section of the Old Testament is called KETHUBIM or THE WRITINGS and consists of twelve books. These books come from different times and places and, at first sight, would appear to have nothing in common. The librarian might be tempted to name the section Bits & Pieces. But there is a common strand running through most, if not all, of this disparate collection. The common theme is wisdom. One way or another, each of these books helps its readers to put on the mantle of the wise.

KETHUBIM: Where am I going?

There is no belief in eternal reward and punishment, no heaven or hell, in the Old Testament (see below on 1 and 2 Maccabees). Consequently, if God was to mete out reward and punishment, he had to do it during one's life on earth. Some believed that wealth and good health were signs of God's approval. Others felt that the gift of children was a divine reward for virtue and childlessness was seen as a mighty curse and a sure sign that one did not find favour with God. The thinking behind such opinions is evaluated in the BOOK OF JOB and elsewhere in the WRITINGS and found to be wanting.

Another view, and one found in THE WRITINGS, is that wisdom is the pinnacle of human achievement and is the goal toward which God directs his people. King David prayed to be preserved *unto old age and grey hairs* but the wisdom of Solomon, his son, is proverbial.

TWELVE BOOKS OF THE WRITINGS

PSALMS

Name: The Hebrew words means "Songs", even "Songs of Praise".

Date: The Psalms were written by the poets of God's people over a period of a thousand years. The 150 Psalms in TANAK were collected for worship in the Temple built by the exiles who began to trickle back to Jerusalem after 538 B.C.E.

Author: King David and many other unknown men and women.

Summary: The BOOK OF PSALMS is the prayer book of the Jewish people and the Christian Churches. Generation after generation of people who hold the Bible sacred have turned to the Psalms when they wished to talk to God about what matters most. The Psalms are not frivolous prayers. They are not for the mealy-mouthed or the chicken-hearted. The Psalms speak from the human heart to the heart of God. The fool says in his heart, *There is no God*. The wise pray.

Name: Named from the book's fictional hero, the long-suffering Job.

Date: Behind the BOOK OF JOB lies an older story but our version probably dates from a few hundred years before Jesus – at most.

Author: Unknown but a creative theologian not afraid of the big questions.

Summary: Why do bad things happen to good people? Why do good things happen to bad people? Job and his three friends grapple with the age-old question: Why does a good God tolerate evil since he has the power to stop it? A book for the wise to ponder.

PROVERBS

Name: The BOOK OF PROVERBS is a collection of wise sayings, moral maxims and proverbs.

Date: In its present form the book probably dates from the fifth century before Jesus but many of the sayings it enshrines are as old as the hills.

Author: The collector of PROVERBS is unknown, though the Bible champions Solomon. The book distills some of the human wisdom attained by men and women throughout the ancient Middle East.

Summary: PROVERBS is essentially a worldly and practical book. Wisdom is not some airy-fairy speculation but hard won insights into how to cope with life: *Blessed is the one who finds wisdom ... for the gain of it is better ... than gold.* There is much about the responsibilities of parents, the duties of children: *A wise son makes a glad father.* The wisdom of PROVERBS is practical wisdom.

RUTH

Name: Named after the heroine Ruth, a pagan woman from Moab (Jordan). She may have been an historical figure since she is named as the great-grandmother of King David but the author has fictionalised her story.

Date: A matter of dispute but likely to come from the century after the return from exile.

Author: Unknown but a writer of genius. The BOOK OF RUTH is very beautiful.

Summary: *A woman of worth*, Ruth marries an exile from Bethlehem who dies. She goes back with Naomi, her mother-in-law, to Bethlehem and there meets Boaz, a mature but wealthy farmer, who discovers that Naomi is a distant relative and that he is obligated to her family. He falls in love with Ruth and ... well, read on!

SONG OF SONGS

Name: The name means "the best of all songs" (cf. "the holy of holies"). Sometimes it is called THE SONG OF SOLOMON.

Date: The SONG OF SONGS comes from after the exiles' return, probably from somewhere around 400 B.C.E.

Author: The opening line identifies King Solomon as the author but this is no more than an author claiming royal patronage.

Summary: The SONG OF SONGS is one of the world's great love poems. A man and a woman delight in their deep love and the sexual union created by their love. The poem is made up of alternative voices, now the man, now the woman, speaking of their longing for each other.

QOHELET (ECCLESIASTES)

Name: The word *qohelet* is not a name but a common noun referring to "one who addresses the assembly of the people". The Greek word for assembly is *ekklesia* and this gives us the Latin and English title ECCLESIASTES. The word is usually translated "the preacher".

Date: Though the work deals with issues that have always preoccupied humanity, this collection of wise reflection is thought to have been assembled in the third century B.C.E.

Author: Unknown. The opening verse claims that The Preacher is in fact the son of King David, that is, Solomon. But this is no more than an attempt to send the book into the world with a "big" name attached to it.

Summary: *Vanity of vanities!* The Preacher has a pessimistic view of life. There is no hope of a hereafter, the good and evil both die and in this life the evil frequently prosper. Knowledge, pleasure, wealth, even love are of no account. God has put eternity into people's thoughts but that is another illusion. There is nothing better than to eat, drink and enjoy oneself as best one can. To be comfortable is to be wise.

LAMENTATIONS

Name: LAMENTATIONS is the name given to five poems which were used to lament the sacking of the city of Jerusalem, the destruction of the first Temple and the exiling of the people of Judah in 586 B.C.E.

Date: Somewhere between the events of 586 B.C.E. and the return from exile.

Author: Some suggest Jeremiah (the Greek and English Bibles attach the laments to JEREMIAH) but this is extremely unlikely.

Content: LAMENTATIONS consists of four poetical laments concerning the events of 586 B.C.E. and a fifth which a prayer for deliverance. The poems have a rather artificial alphabetical arrangement which detracts from their profound purpose.

ESTHER

Name: The book is named after its fictional heroine, a Jewish young woman who became a queen.

Date: A Greek version of the BOOK OF ESTHER existed in 114 B.C.E. and we may assign the Hebrew original to a generation or two before that.

Author: Unknown. The events recorded in the book are said (doubtfully) to have initiated the Feast of Purim.

Summary: A young Jewish woman finds herself in the harem of the Persian king and becomes queen. When an evil prime minister persuades the king to exterminate all Jews within his realm, Esther and her uncle Mordecai foil the plot and turn the tables. A gory short novel.

DANIEL

Name: Named after the book's principal character.

Date: The historical background to the BOOK OF DANIEL establishes that it must have been written between 167 and 164 B.C.E.

Author: While the book is accredited to Daniel, we know nothing of him apart from the information found therein.

Summary: In the first part of the book Daniel and his three friends are in service to King Nebuchadnezzar of Babylon. Fidelity to their Jewish faith lands them in the fiery furnace, from which they are miraculously delivered. Further adventures leads our hero to the lion's den and deliverance causes all to glorify God. The second part of the book is devoted Daniel's vision of God's future victory over those who exploit his people. The beginnings of a theology of life with God after death may be detected here.

1 and 2 CHRONICLES

The books 1 and 2 Chronicles, Ezra and Nehemiah are grouped together because they originally formed one work of a single author. They are concerned with the affairs of Judah, the southern kingdom, for the most part. They come from Jerusalem and are concerned with the religious rehabilitation of the people, the reconstruction of Jerusalem and its Temple and the encouragement of the faithful to persevere so that God's will may be done in their regard and for the benefit of all humanity.

Name: The BOOKS OF CHRONICLES are so named because they chronicle the "history" of the monarchy (mainly of Judah) from the time of David to its end.

Date: Most likely CHRONICLES come from the third century B.C.E. when Judah was undergoing a brief period of relative freedom, a fact which accounts for the work's optimism.

Author: Unknown but the contents suggest a Jerusalem priest, a monarchist and an optimist.

Summary: The long genealogy opening the work provides continuity with the past and a belief in God's consistent and irrevocable attachment to his people. The story of David is told omitting all his sins (no adultery with Bathsheba, for example). David is the architect, Solomon the builder, of the Temple. Other kings, except Hezekiah and Josiah, are apostates and the destruction of Jerusalem and exile inevitable. The idealised picture of the past provides a blueprint for the future. The institutions of the royal house of David and the priesthood of the Temple are seen as the instruments of future national rehabilitation.

EZRA and NEHEMIAH

Name: The books are named after the architects of the reconstruction Temple and city after the return, Ezra the scribe and Nehemiah the builder.

Date: As for CHRONICLES.

Author: As for CHRONICLES.

Summary: On their return, the people seek to rebuild the Temple and the city. Their efforts are constantly frustrated by Samaritans. Alongside the physical restoration, their leaders try to rehabilitate the faith of the people. For these architects of renewal there are three pillars of Judaism: the Jews are God's chosen people (no intermarriage), the Law is their protective shield, the Temple their house of God.

A SUMMARY OF TANAK

The TORAH establishes the identity of a religious Jew. All humanity comes from God but one people is called to carry God's holy Law. This is both a gift and a burden. Many seek to throw off the burden and the role of the PROPHETS is to call faithless ones to repentance, to implore steadfastness in the midst of adversity, to point to a glorious future. The WRITINGS seek to discern the future and, failing to find an after-life with God, declare that wisdom is the goal. And that is what TANAK is about: live TORAH, listen to the PROPHETS and you will become wise with the wisdom to be found in the WRITINGS.

Miscellaneous
or Apocryphal Books

A number of books will be found in bibles belonging to Christians of the Orthodox and Catholic Churches. Churches of the Reformation follow the list of books according to the Jewish Bible (TANAK). Some books found in ancient Greek versions of the Bible but not in the original Hebrew are regarded by Catholic and Orthodox as authentic and part of Scripture. Traditionally called APOCRYPHA (Hidden Writings), our librarian may wish to put these disputed works on a shelf headed "Miscellaneous" for they are a mixed bag.

SEVEN APOCRYPHAL BOOKS

TOBIT

Name: Named after its Jewish hero, living in exile in Nineveh.

Date: Probably written in Egypt three or four hundred years before the days of Jesus.

Author: Unknown. Cavalier with history and geography.

Summary: Tobit's friend, Raguel, has a daughter whose seven bridegrooms are killed by an evil spirit on her wedding nights. Tobit's son, guided by the angel Raphael, marries Sarah and survives. A fictional story, enshrining domestic values.

JUDITH

Name: Named after its Jewish heroine Judith, a beautiful, young and resourceful widow. The book is a work of fiction.

Date: Probably written in the century before Jesus.

Author: Unknown.

Summary: In this gory fiction, an imaginary Jewish capital city is besieged by evil Holofernes, the Assyrian commander. The inhabitants cower but Judith puts on the style, goes to Holofernes' tent, and, while he seeks to seduce her, she cuts off his head. Assyrians flee in fear and everyone lives happily ever after.

1 and 2 MACCABEES

Name: The title of the two BOOKS OF MAC-CABEES is derived from the name Maccabaeus, given to a certain Judas, the central character of the story, a name passed on to his brothers who also distinguish themselves in upholding the rights of their people against enemies.

Date: Probably written within a hundred years before the birth of Jesus. The events recorded take place following the accession of the cruel Antiochus

Epiphanes (175 B.C.E.) down to the death of Simon Maccabee in 134 B.C.E.

Author: Unknown.

Summary: The first book deals with the fate of those Jews who resist the inroads of foreign influences (in this case, Hellenism) on their way of life. The Maccabee family resist the cultural and military domination of Antiochus Epiphanes and fight for freedom. The second book, a rambling affair, deals with some of the events of the first. It aims to encourage Jews in Alexandria (Egypt) to support the fight in Palestine and to honour the Temple. Teaching on the resurrection of the dead, praying for the dead and eternal reward and punishment, confer interest on an otherwise boring book.

BARUCH

Name: Named after the alleged author who claims to have written the work in Babylon after the Chaldeans had destroyed Jerusalem (586 B.C.E.).

Date: The book contains a collection of pieces from differing times. Some parts may go back to the days of exile in Babylon, others some hundreds of years later.

Author: Unknown.

Summary: The book contains a prayer of the people repenting their rejection of the TORAH and begging forgiveness and a return to the land. A long hymn to Wisdom defines it as TORAH. A personified Jerusalem laments its sorrows and hopes for mercy. A letter purporting to come from Jeremiah is appended.

WISDOM

Name: Sometimes called THE WISDOM OF SOLOMON, this book is an exposition of the nature of wisdom according to an Alexandrian Jew.

Date: The book comes from the Jewish community in Alexandria and was written about fifty years before Jesus was born.

Author: The attribution to King Solomon is an attempt to cast over itself the mantle of the (allegedly) wisest man of all. The writer is clearly a Jew who has contact with Greek culture and is sympathetic towards it but wishes to uphold his own inheritance.

Summary: The BOOK OF WISDOM maintains that wisdom dwelt with God from eternity and is given to humanity for its guidance. The worldly may reject wisdom but the humble will (and this is new) reap eternal life (*the souls of the virtuous are in the hands of God*). Like Solomon, all must seek and pray for wisdom, the greatest of all gifts.

ECCLESIASTICUS

Name: The name ECCLESIASTICUS seems to spring from the Church's frequent use of the work (ekklesia = church assembly). It is also called SIRACH or the WISDOM OF JESUS BEN SIRACH.

Date: While internal evidence suggests a date around 190 B.C.E., the work was translated by Sirach's grandson sixty years later. Some have suggested a date after the time of Jesus.

Author: The book is a translation by his grandson of a work written by Jesus ben Sirach carried out in Egypt in the thirty-eight year of the reign of King Euergetes (170-117 B.C.E.).

Summary: ECCLESIASTICUS is a hymn to wisdom. *The fear of the Lord is the beginning of wisdom.* Duty to parents, care for the poor, prudence and common sense, mark one who would be wise. There is advice for parents, children, priests, women and on the place of all in God's scheme of things.

A SUMMARY OF APOCRYPHAL BOOKS

The books on our miscellaneous shelf, along with some questions and speculation in other Old Testament books, begin to question the traditional belief that there is no life with God after death, even for those who live holy lives. We can see emerging the idea that, at least for very virtuous defenders of God's good name, such as the Maccabee brothers, there will be vindication in eternity. There is as yet no straightforward belief in heaven and hell, no clearcut understanding of the resurrection of the body on the last day. But seeds have been planted and, in God's good time, they will grow.

Between the Old and the New Testaments

Not all early Christian writings became part of the New Testament. Similarly, not all Jewish writings before the time of Jesus made it into the Old Testament. Yet such writings are of immense importance and that for two reasons. First, they witness to an ongoing reflection on deep religious matters, often advancing positions held in the Old Testament. This is clear in the endeavour to clarify belief in life with God after death. Secondly, such writings help to bridge what may seem to be gaps between the thought of the Old and of the New Testaments. Sometimes ideas in the New Testament seem to spring from nowhere – a perplexing example is the idea that Christ descended into hell (1 Peter 3:19) – but careful attention to developing Jewish thought outside the Bible often puts such apparently novel ideas into perspective.

Some writings which come from the centuries immediately before the coming of Jesus are of particular importance. The most famous and by far the most significant are the writings which come from the people who founded a religious community on the shores of the Dead Sea at a place called in Arabic Qumran.

SCROLLS FROM THE DEAD SEA

About one hundred and fifty years before the time of Jesus a movement developed in Judaism concerned to bring about a religious reformation. Shunning the path of revolutionary nationalism, the movement looked to the books of TANAK, to the word of God, to seek there a way for the future. Eventually, a leader arose who was impressed by the necessity of going into the desert to rediscover God. The Teacher of Righteousness, as he came to be called, led his followers to the desert beside the Dead Sea and there set up a community dedicated to preparing for a new religious reformation.

The community devoted itself to studying TANAK for they believed that what God had done in the past would reveal a blueprint for his future action. Copies of the sacred texts were painstakingly produced. The rules and aspirations of the community were carefully recorded. All together an incredible body of writing was produced.

Before the community was finally destroyed by the Romans in 70 C.E., it hid its treasures and in 1947 a shepherd boy stumbled on what has become known as THE DEAD SEA SCROLLS. Subsequent excavations have unearthed as many as 800 manuscripts. About a quarter of these are copies of books of the Bible, as much again are commentaries on the sacred books. A large portion is given over to the rule of the community which was to transform its adherents into God's instrument in the creation of a new and purified people of Israel. Converts to the community were instructed in the TORAH as expounded by the Teacher of Righteousness and baptised and, after a further probation period, were admitted to full membership.

Scholars are discovering many connections between the teaching of Jesus and of the early developments within Christianity and the religious teaching and practices of the monastery at Qumran. Such discoveries warn us that the New Testament for all its originality, does not come out of the blue. Of course, it is built on the understanding of God to be found in the Old Testament. But it comes, too, out of the rich and plenteous store of religious ideas and movements which enriched the world into which Jesus of Nazareth was born.

THE NEW TESTAMENT

We have explored ROOM A of our Bible Library. Now we make our way to another room. We might note that it is not part of the original building but is a most tasteful extension, incorporating the beauty of the original with some new and daring features of its own. It is not an extension which can stand on its own. Its foundations are those of the mother building.

ROOM B: THE NEW TESTAMENT

The books in this room were written within a hundred years after the death of Jesus. Whereas the books of the Old Testament are about a people, we might say that the books of the New Testament are about a person. All of them spring from the life and teaching of Jesus of Nazareth. The movement which Jesus inspired came to be known as Christianity and the writings which make up the New Testament or New Covenant (the Jesus covenant as distinct from the Moses covenant) were written by people committed to that movement. Moreover, they were written about and for that movement. What we have in the New Testament is a running commentary on the thoughts and aspirations, disappointments and hopes of Christians of the first one hundred years of Christian faith.

All of the twenty seven books of the New Testament were written in Greek, the *lingua franca* of the Roman empire into which Christianity was born.

’Εν ἀρχῇ ἦν ὁ Λόγος, καὶ ὁ Λόγος ἦν ·
πρὸς τὸν Θεόν, καὶ Θεὸς ἦν ὁ Λόγος. οὗτος
In the beginning was the word, and the word was
with God, and the word was God

John 1:1

Most of them were written by Jews. It is important
to remember that Jesus was a Jewish layman, belonging to the Jewish faith and that he died with a Jewish
prayer on his lips. We must, remember, too, that all
his earliest followers were Jews, that Jews determined
the basic teaching and structure of Christianity. Even
though New Testament writers wrote in the language
of the empire, rather than in their native Aramaic (a
form of Hebrew), they wrote out of their Jewish inheritance. Particularly, they wrote out of their religious experience as Jews. They did not leave aside
their holy Scripture when they became followers of
Jesus. Rather they saw in Jesus the fulfillment of all
the longings expressed by their prophets in their Bible. TANAK, for early Christian writers, was the birth-
place, not only of Jesus, but of the Jesus' movement.

Room B is divided into three sections. We may
compare the sections of the New Testament with those
of the Old.

TORAH	GOSPELS
PROPHETS	LETTERS
WRITINGS	WRITINGS

The FOUR GOSPELS may be viewed as the Christian TORAH. The GOSPELS are the foundation documents of Christianity. They identify who Jesus is and,

72

by so doing, identify that to which the Christian is called. To be a disciple of Jesus is to attempt to take on his identity, to adopt his concerns, to live by his values. In the GOSPELS would-be followers of Jesus discover who they are called to be. They discover the whys and wherefores of faith.

FOUR GOSPELS

While the GOSPELS are concerned with the identity of Jesus, they are not biographies. They are pictures of how particular communities interpreted Jesus for their time and their place. Gospel-makers did not start with Jesus. They started with certain problems and difficulties within their communities or in their relations with those outside. Then they bring to bear on their problems and difficulties their understanding of Jesus. By selecting stories about Jesus from the Christian treasury and placing them in a particular order and context they present those aspects of the person and teaching of Jesus most likely to meet the needs of their communities. Consequently, the GOSPELS were not written for us. They were written for little groups of Christians of long ago and far away. But Christian peoples down through the ages have seen in them a rule and guide for faith. If we listen to what the GOSPELS have to say to the communities out of which they came, then, we will be able to apply what we hear to our time and our place.

GOSPEL: What is it?

The word "gospel" means "good news". It is not a very common word in ancient Greek. It originally referred to good news of a victory in battle and this is how we might understand it. The GOSPELS are good

74

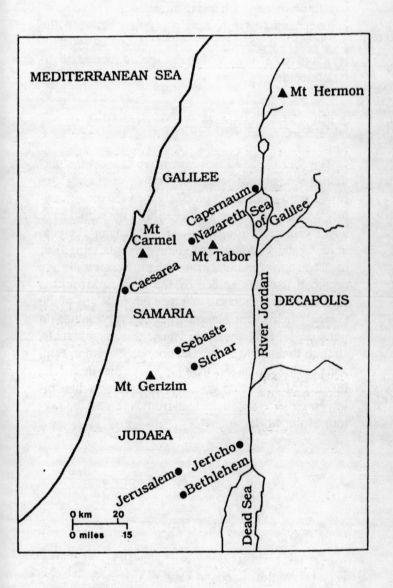

news for they provide accounts of the victory of Jesus, through his death and resurrection, over all powers opposed to God. We distinguish between the gospel of Jesus and books called GOSPELS, each of which gives a version of the gospel to meet particular concerns.

GOSPELS: For whom?

The four GOSPELS were written to meet the particular needs of Christians of far away and long ago. If we could reconstruct precisely the kind of community which gave rise to each GOSPEL, we would have a vital clue to their meaning. At best, we must engage in historical searching and some good guessing. But the Christian community through the ages has always regarded itself as guided by the Holy Spirit and is confident enough to say that its interpretations of the Gospels, while not always right in every detail, do not stray far from the truth. Thus, these ancient texts, strange though they are, can nourish Christian faith and provide for readers today indelible pictures of the identity of Jesus and go far to explain why his followers came to see in the man from Nazareth the saviour of the world.

FOUR BOOKS OF GOSPELS

MATTHEW

Name: The earliest titles given to the GOSPELS were very brief and of second century origin. Thus, *Ac-*

cording to Matthew is as close as we get to a title. It is noticeable that the early manuscripts are not headed *The Gospel of Matthew*. The writers of the GOSPELS are not inventors or creators. The "good news" is of Jesus Christ. The gospel is, first and foremost, the word from Jesus and about Jesus. Jesus is the gospel of God. The written GOSPELS are interpretations of that original. Thus the name *According to Matthew* reveals that a certain Matthew presents his understanding of Jesus of Nazareth. Of itself, it tells us nothing about Matthew.

Date: Dating the GOSPELS is very difficult for one is trying to identify the historical circumstances which caused each GOSPEL to be produced. The *Gospel according to Matthew* incorporates almost all of the *Gospel according to Mark* and it is almost certain that Matthew had a copy of Mark before him as he wrote. So Matthew is later than Mark. From various hints in his story, we might surmise that he wrote after the destruction of Jerusalem and the Temple (70 C.E.), probably five or ten years afterwards.

Author: We know little about the writers of the four GOSPELS. Their names were not attached to the GOSPELS until about one hundred years after they were written. At that late stage, the best Christians could do was guess. Matthew would appear to have been an educated Jew who lived in a Christian community which was made up of Jewish people and Gentile or non-Jewish people. He is not to be identified with the tax collector named Matthew. It is unlikely that the author of the GOSPEL ever met Jesus.

Summary: The *Gospel according to Matthew* was written somewhere in Lebanon or Syria and appears to have been written for a community of Jewish Christians who were admitting pagan Gentiles into their ranks and wondering how to cope with the newcomers who did not have the rich religious traditions of Judaism behind them. Matthew begins his story with the Jewish family tree of Jesus, stretching back through King David to Jacob and Isaac and Abraham himself. But there are foreign, pagan women in the family tree of Jesus: Tamar, Rahab, Ruth and Uriah's wife. At the end of the story, Jesus gives his disciples the task of teaching all nations (Matthew 28:20). In between the first and last chapters Matthew explains, by means of story and sermon, how the Jewish family of Jesus can and must extend into the Gentile family of the Church. The story of the Canaanite woman (Matthew 15:21-28) perfectly illustrates the issues at stake in the *Gospel according to Matthew*.

MARK

Name: The shortest of the GOSPELS is accredited to Mark. Mark, a Latin name, was the most common name in the Roman empire. Thus, of itself, *according to Mark* tells us very little.

Date: Mark probably wrote his GOSPEL in Rome some years after the persecution of Nero who blamed Christians for burning the city of Rome in 64 C.E.

Author: The name Mark occurs eight times in the New Testament but we cannot be sure whether all refer to the same man. Later Christian tradition lumped them all together and came up with a satisfying but wholly unreliable portrait of the author of the Gospel. One tradition holds that Mark was a disciple of Peter who acted as Peter's interpreter in Rome and who wrote down the gist of the apostle's preaching. Some of this may be reliable.

Summary: Mark wrote for a Christian community undergoing or recovering from persecution. Moreover, that Christian community was partly responsible for its woes. When Nero began to round up Christians, we know that some betrayed their fellow Christians to the authorities. Mark wrote for this devastated community in order to rehabilitate its faith. That is why the cross looms large on every page and why the betrayal and death of John the Baptist, the betrayal and death of Jesus and the prediction of Jesus that his followers would suffer betrayal are the very meat of the GOSPEL. Mark seems to be saying that betrayal will infect discipleship but that Jesus can overcome even that virulent disease and restore faith.

LUKE

Name: The third GOSPEL is named after Luke. A certain Luke is mentioned three times in the New Testament as a companion of St Paul and on one occasion he is called a medical doctor.

Date: Luke used Mark's GOSPEL and, possibly, Matthew's. He seems to be writing for a group of Christians who have a fairly peaceful and stable existence. He displays a touching reverence for the Temple which would suggest he wrote after it was destroyed and before it had ceased to have significance for Christians. A date between 75 and 90 C.E. would fit the little evidence we have.

Author: The traditional view is that Luke, a Gentile convert to Christianity, was a companion of St Paul (for a short time), and that he wrote his GOSPEL to expound Paul's understanding of Christianity. There is some evidence that he was a native of Philippi (Macedonia) and wrote his GOSPEL in the Syrian city of Antioch. But Luke's presentation of the Christian gospel little resembles that of Paul and we might conclude that, while Luke may have been a companion of Paul, he little understood the thinking of his friend. Luke also wrote the ACTS OF THE APOSTLES (see below).

Summary: Luke's is a Gospel of prayer, joy and peace. It opens with a man at prayer and with the joyous birth of two babies. It is full of stories of ne'er-do-wells who are given new hope. Its stories are the most memorable in the New Testament: the parables of the Prodigal Son and the Good Samaritan, the healing of the Ten Lepers, the domestic arrangements of Martha and Mary, Zacchaeus climbing a tree. It is a GOSPEL which champions the poor and calls the rich to account. Luke's GOSPEL is at home in the everyday life of Jewish faith and it relishes in its inheritance from Judaism just as it celebrates all that is new in Jesus Christ.

JOHN

Name: The GOSPEL ACCORDING TO JOHN is named after John. But who is this man? Is he John the brother of James and son of Zebedee? Is he the strange figure called in the GOSPEL "the beloved disciple" but otherwise unnamed? Is he John the apostle who sometimes accompanies Peter in the ACTS OF THE APOSTLES? Is he the author of the LETTERS OF JOHN and the BOOK OF REVELATION? Are all these people the same person?

Date: JOHN seems to come out of a Christian community which is having great difficulties with its neighbours in the synagogue. There would appear to be much enmity between Jews and Christians who meet in the pages of this GOSPEL. Historically, this hostility came to a head near 90 C.E. when Jewish authorities decided that Jewish Christians should be banned from the synagogue and, effectively, ostracised by their fellow Jews. The FOURTH GOSPEL reflects that sad break between mother and child and the animosities which surrounded it. A date towards the end of the century is the most likely.

Author: There are numerous oddities in JOHN. It has a fine ending at 20:30-31 but adds another chapter. It begins with a mighty prologue about the Word and never mentions the matter again. It says Jesus baptised some people and then it flatly denies it. In other words, it is difficult to see how this text was produced by one person with a single viewpoint. Rather, it would appear that this GOSPEL has been edited many times by different people.

Summary: The fundamental theme in the GOSPEL is that Jesus has come from God his Father into the world of sin and disobedience and called a community to which he promises to send the Holy Spirit who will preserve it in fidelity to the word and work of Jesus. The great events, such as the healing of the Blind Man and the raising of Lazarus from the dead, are signs of the divine authority of Jesus revealing to all with eyes to see the glory of God shining through the acts of his Son. The GOSPEL (as do the others) so tells stories about Jesus and present his teaching as to address, not the past days when Jesus lived, but the issues which confronted its readers in the last days of the first century of our era.

A SUMMARY OF THE GOSPELS

The GOSPELS are the foundational documents of Christianity. They provide all Christians with images of Jesus which caught the imagination of the earliest Christians and which have molded faith ever since. Each GOSPEL has its own individual insight into the personality of Jesus and the significance of his teaching. All declare that, with the coming of Jesus, God has begun his final intervention in human affairs. The words of the ancient prophets have come to pass and *the day of the Lord* has dawned. The GOSPELS speak of *the kingdom of God*. The message of Jesus is that the kingdom is drawing near in his actions and teaching. He urges his followers to pray that the kingdom will come. The kingdom is not a place; rather, it is an atmosphere, a prevailing condition. The kingdom is none other than *the day of the Lord,* the time when humanity will hear the word of God and keep it. The GOSPELS are TORAH for Christians. The GOSPELS tell Christians who they are, why they are and to what destiny they are called.

Section two
LETTERS

The first documents collected by early Christians were the LETTERS of St Paul and other notable persons of the first generation of Christianity. Of the twenty-seven books in the New Testament, twenty-one are letters. Of these, thirteen are alleged to have been written by St Paul, though we can be certain of only seven. Letters are, for the most part, private matters. They deal with personal things and do not have to be well organised. Friends who know us can fill in the gaps we leave in our letters. As many of the letters in the New Testament are private, at least in the sense that they come from one person to a group of friends, they will often perplex readers, just as any private correspondence will, if we don't know the parties involved. A letter may be written in answer to a question. We will have difficulty in understanding the answer if we do not know (and we often don't) the question. The LETTERS of the New Testament invite the most careful scrutiny and, often enough, create the deepest bafflement.

LETTERS: Why letters?

The LETTERS of the New Testament are like the PROPHETS of the Old Testament. They provide a running commentary on how various groups are living up to their new faith. They admonish, warn, counsel, direct and cosset new communities of Christians. They answer queries and dispel anxieties. As Isaiah and Jeremiah at once warn of infidelity to the TORAH and encourage new faithfulness to its demands, so Paul and James and the rest beg their converts to be true to Jesus and to his way and spell out the consequences of lapsing from the gospel truth they have embraced. Like the ancient prophets who spoke the word of the LORD, the letter writers of the New Testament treat of everyday occurrences amidst the turmoil of history. As the prophets of old sought to protect little Israel from the evil world all around, so the LETTERS sought to protect littlegroups of Christians scattered throughout the Roman empire as so many oases of faith in a desert of paganism. As the great preachers of the gospel, Paul and the rest, traversed the eastern empire spreading the word, they kept in touch with their little flocks by letter. It is these LETTERS which keep today's Christians in touch with the fathers and mothers of our faith.

First shelf: Paul's Letters

LETTER TO THE ROMANS

Name: Paul did not found the Christian community in Rome. But his longest and most formal letter was directed to Christians in the capital city of the empire. Christians in the capital were mostly Gentiles but there were Jewish Christians among them.

Date: Dating New Testament documents is a hazardous activity. Many would agree that Paul wrote his letter in the winter of 57/58 C.E. while resident in Corinth. With good weather, it only took ten days for a letter to reach Rome from Corinth!

Author: Paul was a Jew, probably born in the cultured city of Tarsus (in modern southeast Turkey), at a guess ten years after the birth of Jesus. He was called by the Jewish name Saul but, as was often the case, he was also given a Roman name, Paul. He was brought up in the strict Jewish tradition of the Pharisees and well educated (partly, in Jerusalem). He seems to have been a supporter of early opposition to Christians within Judaism and to have accepted responsibility for their suppression. On his way to Damascus to arrest some Christians, he had an experience of the risen Lord which forced him to see that Jesus was the fulfillment of all that he stood for as a devout Jew. He was baptised in Damascus and spent three years in Arabia (on retreat in the desert?) before embarking on the great missionary journeys in Asia Minor and Greece which did so much to spread the gospel from the confines of Palestine to the great cities of the empire. Paul is the great intellectual genius of the early Church.

Summary: ROMANS is a public letter, directed to Gentile and Jewish Christians in Rome, to introduce himself to a church he did not found and to seek support for his proposed mission to Spain. He writes gently to intervene in difficulties between Gentile and Jewish Christians concerning certain dietary disputes. He spells out his understanding of the gospel: *the righteous live by faith*. It is Jesus Christ, not the Law enshrined in TORAH, which brings salvation to all human beings, Jew and Gentile alike. It is God's love, God's graciousness through faith in Jesus Christ, not human effort, which brings all who are sinners home.

THE FIRST LETTER TO THE CORINTHIANS

Name: 1 CORINTHIANS is, like all Paul's letters, named after its destination, the Christian community in the notoriously wild port of Corinth. Paul (with Prisca and Aquila) founded the Church there and had a particular affection for this exasperating but utterly lovable community of enthusiastic Christians.

Date: The LETTERS of St Paul are not listed in the New Testament according to date with, as we might expect, the earliest first and the latest, last. They are arranged according to length. ROMANS is the longest and PHILEMON the shortest. 1 CORINTHIANS was written in Ephesus, probably when he returned there in 54 C.E.

Author: St Paul. He associates his friend Sosthenes with the letter.

Summary: Hearing that there were dissensions in the community, Paul writes to remind them of the really important things: they are saved by a wise God who does not offer dazzling displays of power but his Son on a cross, Christ crucified. All must imitate the slave status of Jesus Christ. Such is their dignity before God that they must shun all immorality, the married in their state, the unmarried in theirs. Elements of pagan worship are to be avoided, the Eucharist celebrated with dignity, and love placed at the centre of all things.

The one body of the Church has many parts but each must work for all because all are one in Christ.

THE SECOND LETTER TO THE CORINTHIANS

Name: Three letters of Paul to Corinth have been lost. It is not clear where in the series this letter should be placed.

Date: The letter comes a short time after the first and may have been written from Macedonia in 58 C.E.

Author: Paul who associates Timothy with the letter.

Summary: Paul reflects on his role as an apostle, sharing his most intimate thoughts on his vocation with his Corinthian brothers and sisters. As God was in Christ reconciling the world to himself, so Paul has received the call to spread the message of reconciliation as an ambassador of Christ. He begs for alms for impoverished Jerusalem Christians. He concludes with an account of his ministry among the Corinthians and an admission of the special place they have in his heart.

THE LETTER OF PAUL TO THE GALATIANS

Name: Paul founded the community in Galatia, a province in central Asia Minor (Turkey), on his second missionary journey.

Date: Probably written in 54 C.E. when Paul was resident in Ephesus, spending some time in prison.

Author: Paul. An angry Paul.

Summary: Galatians is an angry letter. Paul had always insisted that faith, not observing the minutiae of Jewish laws, must be the hallmark of believers in the salvation won by Christ Jesus. He rebukes Peter (Cephas) and all backsliders who want to change the freedom of the gospel for the shackles of law. For Paul, the gospel makes Jew and pagan, slaves and free-born, women and men, equal in God's sight for all are redeemed in Jesus. All are called to freedom, not legal entanglement. Paul begs his "foolish Galatians" to live in love, joy, peace, patience, kindness, goodness, faithfulness, gentleness and self-control.

THE LETTER OF PAUL TO THE EPHESIANS

Name: The letter takes its name from the important city of Ephesus on the west coast of Asia Minor, where Paul had laboured and had his difficulties (Acts 19:23-41 and 20:17-35).

Date: The dating of EPHESIANS depends on whether it is regarded as having been written by Paul or is the work of an anonymous disciple of the apostle. If Paul is the author, it may have been written while he was under house arrest in Rome in 61/63 C.E. Otherwise, a date between 70 and 100 C.E. is suggested.

Author: This is a matter of much dispute since the style and teaching of EPHESIANS differs markedly from Paul's undoubted writings. While a writer may adopt more than one style, it is the (alleged) lack of connection between the thought of EPHESIANS and

Paul's earlier thinking that makes Pauline authorship doubtful. However, one may have new thoughts and insights and require a new style to express them.

Summary: A great mystery has been revealed: it is God's eternal will to save Gentiles as well as Jews. Death on the cross has made peace between pagan and Jew. All sinners are forgiven and there is now but one "person", the whole of redeemed humanity. The Church, the one, holy, apostolic and Catholic Church is sign of humanity's new oneness; it is the bride of Christ. This exalted status demands a life of peace, harmony and good social order.

THE LETTER OF PAUL TO THE PHILIPPIANS

Name: On his first excursion into Europe, Paul founded churches at Neapolis, Philippi and Thessalonica, all in Macedonia.

Date: Probably written while Paul was in prison in Rome (61-63 C.E.). The letter mentions an imprisonment, a praetorium and Caesar's household which suggest an imperial setting.

Author: Paul. He associates his "brother" Timothy with his letter.

Summary: Paul (as usual) thanks God for the grace he and the Philippians have as recipients of the good news. He prays that they may live up to their high calling, living in peace and harmony and modelling their lives on Jesus Christ who did not exploit his equality with God for self-advantage. Paul's fellow-

workers, Timothy and Epaphroditus, are commended
to the Philippians, whom Paul hopes to visit on re-
lease from prison. The letter is suffused with love,
thanksgiving and joy, hallmarks, Paul advises, of those
blessed by the gospel: *Rejoice in the Lord always;
again I will say, Rejoice!*

THE LETTER OF PAUL TO THE COLOSSIANS

Name: Named after its recipient, the Christian community in the city of Colossae (Asia Minor), founded
by Epaphras, under Paul's direction.

Date: Paul wrote a number of LETTERS while im-
prisoned in Rome (61-63 C.E.), often called "the cap-
tivity epistles", of which this is one.

Author: That Paul wrote COLOSSIANS has often
been doubted for the same reasons as Ephesians (see
above). But there are no insuperable arguments against
Pauline authorship.

Summary: Giving thanks for their great faith, Paul
urges the Colossians to live according to the divine
mercy bestowed on them through the redemption and
forgiveness of sins given them in Christ, *the image
(icon) of the invisible God*. Paul warns them against
a false spirituality (associated with special diets and
devotions) which relies on *principalities and powers*
(super angels) as the lifeline between humanity and
God. Jesus, whose death has made redundant all other
spiritual powers, will come again to bring *all who are
hid with Christ in God* to eternal glory. Accordingly,
Colossians must live Christ-like lives, shunning im-

morality, espousing compassion, meekness and patience. Husbands must love their wives, masters must treat slaves justly, all must be steadfast in prayer.

THE FIRST LETTER OF PAUL
TO THE THESSALONIANS

Name: The letter is addressed to the Church at Thessalonia (modern Salonika) in Macedonia. Paul founded it on his first excursion into Europe (Acts 16-18).

Date: The earliest of Paul's letters to survive, 1 THESSALONIANS was written from Corinth in the winter of 50-51 C.E.

Author: Paul who associates Silvanus and Timothy with the letter.

Summary: Paul thanks God for his converts from paganism who have embraced *the word of God* and now await the second coming of Jesus Christ. He defends his preaching activity in Thessalonica and explains why he sent Timothy to them. He encourages all to live holy lives, especially in sexual matters. Some Thessalonians appear to have thought that, since by baptism they share in the resurrection of Jesus, they would not die. Paul tells them that Christians will die but that they will be raised to glory at the return of Christ. His final word: *Be at peace among yourselves*.

THE SECOND LETTER OF PAUL
TO THE THESSALONIANS

Name: As 1 THESSALONIANS.

Date: About a year after 1 THESSALONIANS.

Author: Paul, again in association with Silvanus and Timothy.

Summary: Having touched on the second coming of Christ and the destiny of Christians in 1 THESSALONIANS, Paul expands on that teaching. *Those who do not know God* will suffer annihilation. Faithful Christians await the coming of our Lord Jesus, an event which will be preceded by certain signs, and disregard false rumours that the end is nigh. The apostle asks for prayers and discourages idleness.

THE LETTER OF PAUL TO PHILEMON

Name: Named after Philemon, the owner of the slave Onesimus. But the letter is also addressed to Philemon, his wife Appia, Archippus and *the church in your house*.

Date: About the same time as EPHESIANS and COLOSSIANS (see above).

Author: Paul who associates Timothy with his letter.

Summary: Onesimus, Philemon's slave, ran away from Colossae and was converted by Paul in Ephesus. The apostle sends the slave back to his master but reminds Philemon that the slave is now a brother in Christ and should be treated accordingly. Paul does not use his authority to compel Philemon but pleads the obligations of friendship. The letter is addressed to the whole community and reveals a true pastor.

Second Shelf : Three Pastoral Letters

THE FIRST LETTER TO TIMOTHY

Name: The letter purports to be from St Paul to Timothy, a co-worker with the apostle in many of his missionary exploits.

Date: Probably written between 85-100 C.E.

Author: The Pastoral Letters, 1 and 2 TIMOTHY and TITUS, so called because they give advice on the exercise of pastoral responsibility, were not written by Paul but by an anonymous Christian who sought to add the weight of the apostle's authority to his own rather pedestrian thinking. The author pretends to write to two of Paul's most trusted co-workers though his message is intended for all the Churches. Personal details relating to Paul are added to make the letters appear genuine.

Summary: The letter presents Paul instructing Timothy to beware of false teachers, to encourage prayer for all and to see that women conduct themselves appropriately. The writer provides instruction for bishops and deacons. All in *the household of God* are enjoined to shun false teachers, to see the goodness of all creation and to uphold marriage. There are detailed instructions for widows, elders, and slaves, with a caution for the rich.

THE SECOND LETTER TO TIMOTHY

Name: See on 1 TIMOTHY above.

Date: See on 1 TIMOTHY above.

Author: See on 1 TIMOTHY above.

Summary: After a thanksgiving section, Paul bequeathes his own faith (for which he had suffered much) to Timothy, exhorting him to endure suffering with similar fortitude, to teach bravely in the face of false teachers, taking courage from Paul's perseverance in the service of the gospel and guidance from his predictions.

THE LETTER TO TITUS

Name: Named after one of Paul's most trusted collaborators, to whom the anonymous author fictitiously addresses his letter.

Date: See on 1 TIMOTHY.

Author: See on 1 TIMOTHY.

Summary: Intended for the instruction of new Jewish communities of Christians in Crete, the writer exhorts Titus to appoint elders and bishops who will champion sound doctrine in the face of worldly uncertainties. Older men and women, younger women and men and slaves are instructed how to behave. Jesus our Saviour is the model for all. Christians are counselled to obey civil authorities and to live useful, generous and peaceful lives as befits those who, through no human merit, are saved by Jesus Christ.

Third Shelf: Eight Pastoral Letters

THE LETTER TO THE HEBREWS

Name: The name is derived from the recipients, an exclusively Jewish Christian community, living, it would seem, in Alexandria (Egypt).

Date: The Jerusalem Temple is a live issue in HEBREWS. It must have been in operation at the time of writing. Had it already been destroyed, as it was in 70 C.E., the author would surely have mentioned the fact. A date shortly before 70 C.E. suggests itself.

Author: An unknown Jew, though Apollo (Acts 18:24-28) and Joseph Barnabas, a Jewish Cypriot (Acts 4:36-37), have been suggested.

Summary: No angel, no Moses, no priest, no Temple, no sacrifice, no covenant, can do what Jesus did. As Son of God, he became human and his death and resurrection established him as our High Priest whose ministry of perpetual prayer before the Father opens salvation to all. He alone has entered the heavenly Holy of Holies, to which he leads all who, like the great ones of old, persevere in faith.

THE LETTER OF JAMES

Name: Named after James, "the brother of the Lord".

Date: JAMES may have been written as early as 49 C.E. and, almost certainly, before 70 C.E.

Author: James, identified as a brother of Jesus in Mark 6:3, leader of the first Christian community in Jerusalem, may not be the author but most agree that the material therein goes back to the teaching of one whom Paul calls an acknowledged pillar of the Church (Galatians 2:9). The excellent Greek of the letter points to the Jewish community in Alexandria as its place of origin.

Summary: JAMES defines religion: to visit orphans and widows in their affliction and to keep oneself unspotted from the world (world, for James, is creation contaminated by misused wealth). His concerns are practical. First, don't be double-minded, going through the motions of religion (in case they might work), yet putting one's real trust in human discretion. Secondly, seek wisdom, which is gentleness, itself open to reason and full of mercy. Thirdly, beware of wealth. Above all, be steadfast in prayer.

THE FIRST LETTER OF PETER

Name: Named after Simon Peter, leader of the Twelve and apostle to the circumcised (Galatians 2:7).

Date: Probably around 80 C.E. though some date it as late as 120 C.E.

Author: Though credited to St Peter, the letter was probably written from Rome by a disciple of the great man who wished his teaching to be of guidance and comfort to Christians of Asia Minor who were suffering harassment from their pagan families and *one-time friends*.

Summary: Thanking God for living hope, founded on the resurrection of Jesus, surpassing the expectation of prophets, the letter commends holiness of life, grounded on God's word. The duties of free citizens, slaves, wives and husbands are outlined (Christ is the example for all). The innocence of the crucified Jesus demands that his followers be innocent before the law and yet steadfast when persecuted. Leaders must model themselves on the chief Shepherd. Eternal glory awaits those who watch. Is this letter an Easter Vigil sermon?

THE SECOND LETTER OF PETER

Name: Named after St Peter, purporting to be a final testament and farewell to all the faithful, as the death of the apostle approaches.

Date: Possibly as late as 120 C.E. and certainly after 96 C.E.

Author: An unknown author has set out to adapt what he thinks to have been the teaching of St Peter to Christians of his generation who are worried by the long delay of the Second Coming of Jesus. He copied much from the LETTER OF JUDE.

Summary: Those who await the coming of our Lord Jesus Christ must conduct themselves accordingly, living lives of faith and love. The prophets pointed to the second coming and, properly interpreted, refute the predictions of immoral false teachers, a breed whose imminent destruction was foreshadowed by the fate of fallen angels and the like. The faithful are exhorted to remain firm in the hope of the imminent return of Jesus, remembering that with the Lord one day is as a thousand years.

THE THREE LETTERS OF JOHN

Name: The LETTERS OF JOHN are interconnected and are named after St John the Apostle.

Date: If the letters were issued later than the GOSPEL OF JOHN, a date after 100 C.E. is likely. They may have been written in Ephesus in response to bitter divisions within the intense but fragile communities the apostle left behind.

Author: These writings are the work of anonymous members of communities tracing their origins to St John. The second and third letters are from an elder or presbyter.

Summary:

THE FIRST LETTER OF JOHN

In the face of dissidents who have left the community because they deny that Jesus is the Messiah

(Christ) and who claim to be without sin, the writer teaches that sin is ever present and ever forgiven, that Jesus died to overcome *the sins of the whole world*. To know this Jesus is to know the Father and the Spirit and to live according to the commandment of love. The false prophets who teach otherwise are antichrists and belong to the world of sin. True believers recognise that *Jesus is the Son of God*.

THE SECOND LETTER OF JOHN

From an anonymous elder to a Christian household, the letter repeats the essential commandment: *love one another*. Anyone who does not acknowledge that Jesus is truly the Messiah and truly a human being is to be rejected.

THE THIRD LETTER OF JOHN

Directed to a certain Gaius, the letter praises his adherence to the truth and begs assistance for fellow workers in the service of God's truth. Diotrephes is condemned. Demetrius is commended. All are enjoined to imitate what is good.

THE LETTER OF JUDE

Name: Named after Judas (not Iscariot), the brother of Jesus and James (Mark 6:3).

Date: As early as 60 C.E. but certainly before SECOND PETER which quotes it.

Author: The very Jewishness of the letter, with its peculiarly Jewish methods of arguing from the Old Testament and other Jewish literature would suggest an anonymous scribe who pinned the prestigious name of a member of the family of Jesus to his exceptional work.

Summary: Warning against certain itinerant charismatics who pervert God's grace into moral license, Judas teaches that such people have been condemned in Scripture and will meet the same fate as unbelievers, fallen angels, Sodom and Gomorrah, Cain and other biblical villains. The apostles themselves condemned such scoffers who follow their own passions. His advice is to live righteous lives, preparing for the coming of our Lord Jesus Christ.

Section three
WRITINGS

The ACTS OF THE APOSTLES marks the beginning of the adventure of the Church. The Holy Spirit, the gift of Jesus, comes to carry on the work begun in creation, nurtured by the witness of the faithful people of Israel and revealed to all humanity in the cross of our Lord Jesus. St Luke moves the little band of disciples from the upper room of fear in the city of Jerusalem, from the first days of startling preaching to the outreach to Gentile people and, finally, to Rome. The message of Jesus is preached from the holy city to the capital city.

The BOOK OF REVELATION is the end of the story. The pain and hurt of the Church, its inner turmoil and persecution from without, are painted in startling, even frightening, images. The last image, the journey's end, is the new Jerusalem, the heavenly city, having the glory of God, its radiance like a most rare jewel (Revelation 21:11).

We might compare these two books with the WRITINGS of the Old Testament. There we learn how to conduct ourselves in the world in order to become wise, in order to reach our destiny. Here we learn how the Church fares in the world and the destiny to which it and all peoples are called.

THE ACTS OF THE APOSTLES

Name: The book records, in a highly selective fashion, some of the missionary activities of the first preachers of the gospel, especially of Peter and Paul. Hence its name.

Date: Between 80 and 90 C.E.

Author: St Luke, author of the GOSPEL OF LUKE.

Summary: The ACTS OF THE APOSTLES plots certain phases in the spread of the gospel. It organises its story around Peter and Paul. The good news is first preached in Jerusalem and spreads, amid difficulties, from there to Samaria and to Syria, on the way facing the momentous decision to admit non-Jews to the new movement. The conversion of Paul and his missionary activities among Gentiles necessitated the important decision concerning the terms on which they were to be admitted. Once decided, ACTS concentrates on the mission of Paul to Asia Minor and into Europe. Finally, he carries the gospel to Rome. The hero of the book is not Peter, not Paul. The hero is the Holy Spirit who causes the message of Jesus to win hearts from little Jerusalem to mighty Rome.

THE REVELATION TO JOHN

Name: The book claims to be an account of revelations given to one called John.

Date: The emperor Domitian reigned from 81 to 96 C.E. and instigated a sporadic persecution of Christians. REVELATION may be a response to this.

Author: The author is not the writer of the GOSPEL OF JOHN. Nor is he one of the Twelve. He is an unknown Christian seer.

Summary: The author calls his work an "apocalypse", a word meaning "revelation" or "disclosure". The revealed secret is about Jesus Christ. He alone is God's champion, empowered to rescue the faithful from an increasingly evil world. The seven churches (symbolising the whole Church) are warned against compromise with the religious, economic and social values of a world destined for divine retribution and ultimate annihilation. The battles between Satan and his earthly minions and the mighty forces of God are described in horrendous images. But for all its bewildering visions REVELATION is like any other book of the Bible. It is an invitation to hear God's call, to respond to it and to live accordingly.

SUMMARY OF THE BOOKS
OF THE NEW TESTAMENT

The four GOSPELS open the call of the New Testament. Built, as they are, on the foundation stone of Israel's faith, they witness to the life and work of a faithful Jew, Jesus of Nazareth. They preach the good news of Jesus *and him crucified*. They call people to live in their time the life Jesus lived in his. *Come, follow me!* That is the Jesus-word addressed to peoples everywhere. The hearing of the word is the beginning of the Church.

The ACTS OF THE APOSTLES tells of the first bold steps of the gospel as it begins to make its way through the world. The first communities (Churches) are formed and, under the guidance of the Holy Spirit, the difficult but inexorable march from Jerusalem to Rome is accomplished.

The LETTERS of Paul and the rest witness to the Church in the world. There it finds its people, poor in spirit, like sheep without a shepherd, and it takes them to the gospel, to the good news of God-caring, the good news of God-saving. They witness, too, to the pain and anguish of new Christians, beset by harassment and dissension. They show us the realities of the Church, a place of squabbling, troublesome people, forever counting angels on pinheads. But they show, too, a people of joy and hope, a people cherishing justice and righteousness, a people building peace, a people engaged in the sublime task of declaring that God is on our side, that there is nothing to fear.

The Bible begins in a new creation and so it ends. The BOOK OF REVELATION seeks to remove the veil, to show where the Creator means to lead his creation, to show where the gospel and its little Churches and, indeed, all peoples, come to rest. Jerusalem is a sign of human desperation: it is the city of crucifixion. But crucifixion is not God's final word in the world. The place of crucifixion itself becomes the place of utter transformation. There will be a new Jerusalem. REVELATION promises that to which all TANAK and all GOSPELS invite suffering humanity:

Behold, the dwelling of God is with people. He will dwell with them, and they shall be his people, and God himself will be with them; he will wipe away every tear from their eyes, and death shall be no more, neither shall there be mourning nor crying nor pain any more, for the former things have passed away.

Revelation 21:3-4

Praying the Bible

Rome wasn't built in a day and the Bible won't be understood in a day. It takes many readings and much pondering before all its many pieces fall into place. Indeed, there is a sense in which we can never fully understand the Scriptures. For one thing, the Bible is God's word in human words and it would be presumptuous, to say the least, to pretend that we could know the mind of God. As St Paul reminds us, *Who has known the mind of the Lord?* (Romans 11:34). Furthermore, human beings and the situations in which they live out their lives change and so it is that the word of God is constantly being addressed to a fluctuating world. To take contrasting examples, the SONG OF SONGS will not speak in the same way to the heart which has fallen in love for the first time and to the heart which knows not only the delights of love but its loss. Parents who have lost a child to drugs or to other prisons of our time will hear the story of the Prodigal Son (Luke 15:11-32) with pain and prayerful hope scarcely comprehensible to those who know no loss.

Yet there is a way into the Bible which keeps us in touch with its moods and tenses and which allows it to move with our changing world. This is the way of prayer. The Bible is, of course, a book of stories but it is also a book of prayers. For centuries the Bible has been the prayer book of the Jewish people who created it and the prayer book of the Church which inherited it. To feel the Bible, to grow to know its heart and soul, it is necessary, at least now and then, to enter into its prayers.

Songs of Praise

The BOOK OF PSALMS, whose Hebrew name means "Songs of Praise", is the great prayer book of the Bible. It provides most of the prayers for public worship in the Jewish synagogue and the Christian Church. The 150 psalms or prayers which we find therein are an excellent map to the heart of the Bible, to the hearts of the people who composed its pages and, indeed, to the heart of God.

Love, hatred, trust, joy, sorrow, anger, pity, hurt, happiness, contentment, rage, gratitude, resentment, despair, hope: such are the realities of human experience and such are the stuff of the Psalms. There is the confident, contented prayer of an unruffled life:

> The LORD is my shepherd, I shall not want;
> he makes me lie down in green pastures.
> He leads me beside still waters;
> he restores my soul.

Psalm 23

There is the fierce prayer of one who is losing hope, whose life is slipping away into despair:

> My God, my God, why have you forsaken me?
> Why are you so far from helping me,
> so far from the words of my groaning?
> O my God, I cry out by day,
> but you do not answer.

Psalm 22

There is the prayer of the one who needs forgiveness and knows the path of repentance:

Have mercy on me, O God,
according to your steadfast love;
according to your abundant mercy
blot out my sins.

Psalm 51

And there is the prayer of praise, the song of a happy heart, the song of a joyful spirit:

O give thanks to the LORD for he is good,
for his steadfast love endures for ever.
O give thanks to the God of gods,
for his steadfast love endures for ever!

Psalm 136

The prayers which make up the BOOK OF PSALMS are as diverse as human emotions. But underlying the diversity is the instinct to pray from where we are. There is no false modesty in the Psalms. Neither is there false piety. When God is present in the calm of our lives, gentle words come naturally. But in the whirlwind, when we feel nothing so strongly as the absence of God, the Psalms help us to shout, to scream, to demand a hearing. Indeed, prayers for all seasons.

Making Prayers

The BOOK OF PSALMS is not the only source of prayers in the Bible. In fact, most books preserve the prayers of the people who fill its pages. Often such prayers are at once ancient and modern:

Our Father who art in heaven,
Hallowed be thy name.
Thy kingdom come.
Thy will be done,
On earth as it is in heaven.
Give us this day our daily bread;
And forgive us our trespasses
As we forgive those who trespass against us.
And lead us not into temptation,
But deliver us from evil.

Matthew 6:9-13

Sometimes they are sadly neglected:

Father,
hallowed be thy name.
Thy kingdom come.
Give us each day our daily bread;
and forgive us our sins,
for we ourselves forgive everyone who is indebted
    to us;
and lead us not into temptation.

Luke 11:2-4

An alternative version of the Bible's most famous prayer!
Here is a bridegroom's prayer:

Blessed are you, O God of our fathers,
and blessed be your holy and glorious name for
    ever.
Let the heavens and all your creatures bless you.
You made Adam and gave him Eve his wife
as a helper and support.
From them the race of humanity has sprung.

110

You said, "It is not good that a man should be alone;
let us make a helper for him like himself".
And now, O LORD I am not taking this sister of
    mine
because of lust, but with sincerity.
Grant that I may find mercy
and may grow old together with her.

Tobit 8:5-7

But there are other prayers which do not fit into
our experience, do not immediately speak to our concerns. There is no need to put such prayers to one
side as alien to our ways. What we must do is adapt.
Here, for example, is a prayer of King Solomon, first
uttered when he was dedicating the Temple in Jerusalem nearly 3,000 years ago:

Now, O my God, let thy eyes be open
and thy ears attentive
to a prayer of this place.
And now arise, O LORD God,
and go to thy resting place,
thou and the ark of thy might.
Let thy priests, O LORD God,
be clothed with salvation,
and let thy saints rejoice in thy goodness,
O LORD God do not turn away the face
of thy anointed one!
Remember thy steadfast love for David
    thy servant.

2 Chronicles 6:40-42

If we use a little imagination we can turn this ancient prayer into a prayer for today:

Now, O my God, let your eyes be open
and your ears attentive
to a prayer from this place.
Let all your priests, O LORD God,
be clothed with salvation.
Let all your people rejoice in your goodness.
O LORD God, do not turn away from us!
Remember your steadfast love for us.
Amen.

Even the BOOK OF REVELATION has beautiful prayers which spring to life with just a modest change or two:

Great and wonderful are your deeds,
O LORD God the Almighty!
Just and true are your ways,
O Ruler of the peoples!
Who shall not reverence and glorify your name,
   O LORD?
All peoples shall come and worship you,
for your justice has been revealed. Amen.
               Adapted from Revelation 15:3-4

We must not be afraid to adapt prayers we find in the Bible to our own words and circumstances. The Bible is a gift to us from a God who spoke of old to our ancestors and who would, through its pages, speak to us. We must use the ancient words and allow them to speak in our time and place. To do so is to pick up the challenge of the Bible. To enter into its prayer is to come to know its God. It is, of course, a risk. To enter into the prayer of the Bible is to risk conversion to its God.

Buying a Bible...

A little history

The first complete translation of the Bible into English was made by John Wycliffe (1330-84). The first printed translation was that of William Tyndale (1494-1536). Both of these were condemned by Church authorities but the Franciscan reawakening of Christianity in the fourteenth century gave rise to a desire for the Bible in the language of everyday speech all over Europe. The Protestant Reformation brought in its train a host of translations. Several were produced in English during the reign of Henry VIII. The Catholic Queen Mary (1553-58) stopped all printing of English Bibles in England but William Whittingham, pastor of the English Church in Geneva, caused an English Bible to be printed in that city. It was dedicated to Queen Elizabeth and became known as the Geneva Bible. It was immensely popular and immensely important. It was the Bible of Shakespeare and Bunyan. It was the Bible which travelled to the New World on the *Mayflower* and it was the Bible Oliver Cromwell read on many a battlefield.

English Catholics were forced to provide themselves with an English Bible and between 1578 and 1610 both the Old and New Testaments were produced at the seminaries of Rheims and Douai by Gregory Martin and Richard Bristow. Bishop Challoner of London revised the Rheims-Douai Bible in 1738 and his revised version remained the Bible of English-speaking Catholics until the 1960s.

When James VI of Scotland became James I of England he ordered that a new translation be made which was to be used in every parish church in the land. In 1611 what became known as the King James Version (KJV) or the Authorised Version (AV) was published. No single book has had so much influence on the development of the English language. A revision of the AV was undertaken in 1870 and completed in 1885. An American edition, which became known as the American Standard Version (ASV) was published in 1901. A further revision, to "embody the best results of modern scholarship as to the meaning of the scriptures", was undertaken in 1937 and completed with a translation of the Apocrypha in 1957. It became known as the Revised Standard Version (RSV) and an edition which included those books which Roman Catholics call deuterocanonical (that is, books belonging to the Bible but of secondary importance) was published in 1977. The RSV was completely revised and issued as the New Revised Standard Version (NRSV) in 1990.

Altogether nearly 250 English translations of all or part of the Bible have been made since 1611. Modern readers have available a host of excellent and relatively cheap translations and revisions. Many of these come from individuals, such as Miles Coverdale (1535), Richard Taverner (the Great Bible of 1539), and Robert Young (1862). In modern times, the translations of James Moffatt (completed 1924), Monsignor Ronald Knox (1955), J. B. Phillips (New Testament, 1958) and William Barclay (New Testament, 1969) have been widely used. All owe their existence to the dedication of those early scholars who strove to place the word of God into the hands of ordinary people.

Some preliminary advice

There are basically two kinds of translation of the Bible available to the modern reader. There are translations which aim to be understood by "the ordinary person in the street" and use a style of language more suitable to private reading than public proclamation in a church. Others try to reproduce the meaning of the original texts as faithfully as possible, even if this leads to some difficulties for the less able reader, while, at the same time, aiming for an ornate style which is well suited to public proclamation. Happily, most modern translations aim to be accurate and accessible to the ordinary reader. Some put more emphasis on accessibility, others on accuracy.

Buying a Bible may be a once-in-lifetime experience for many people. It is, therefore, essential to choose a Bible which suits one's needs. If one wishes to have a Bible which uses ordinary English, such as ordinary people use, then there are translations of this kind available. If one requires a Bible to stimulate private prayer and provide comfort and joy in the quiet moments of life, then a modern ordinary language translation would seem appropriate. If, on the other hand, one wishes to use one's Bible for study, then accuracy of translation and nearness to the original texts, even where this means difficult going in English, will be necessary. Again, a particular translation may seek to serve as a public text, the text to be read in worship. Such a translation must have clarity, dignity of style and a memorable turn of phrase. In other words, there are Bibles for all occasions and it is important to choose one which meets one's needs.

A good Bible should provide more than a good translation of the ancient Hebrew and Greek originals. Many modern Bibles provide good maps, excellent introductions to each section and book of the Bible, as well as detailed and highly informative notes. This is the kind of Bible that provides the reader with the sort of help that it essential if one is coming to it for the first time. Because the books which make up the Bible are two to three thousand years old they are strangers to our time and to our world. We need help to bridge the gap between our century and the centuries from which the Bible emerged. It would be wrong to think (as some people do) that the Bible is easily understood by devout, holy people who receive inspiration from the Holy Spirit to guide them through all difficulties. Piety and the Holy Spirit are no substitute for hard work.

Some people elect to buy only a New Testament. The reasoning here is that the New Testament contains the story of Jesus and of the founding of the Christian Churches. Such readers do not wish to delve into the many writings of the Old Testament with their strange ways and (so it is said) strange God. But such an attitude is erroneous. It is impossible to understand a word of the New Testament without some knowledge of the Old. Consider an iceberg. Nine-tenths of its bulk is hidden beneath the waves, one-tenth visible above the surface. The Old Testament is the nine-tenths, the New Testament the one-tenth. Take away the nine-tenths under the water and the one-tenth sinks without trace to the bottom of the sea. If you know nothing about King David, how can you expect to know anything of the one who is called the Son of

David? Buy a whole Bible, not an incomprehensible New Testament.

A survey

In deciding which Bibles to include in this survey of some of the many excellent translations available today, a few "principles" have been adopted. The first is that the translation should have been made or revised after 1950. Some important and relatively recent archaeological discoveries make this decision necessary. Secondly, translations produced by a group of scholars (preferably, an ecumenical group) will bring more expertise and knowledge to the task than can be achieved by one person working alone. Thirdly, a few Bibles of particular historical importance will be mentioned even though they fall outside one or both of our principles. Also, it is important that potential readers should be aware of the kind of translation offered and whether it comes in American or "English" English. Bibles will be listed according to the year of the publication of both Old and New Testaments.

REVISED STANDARD VERSION

The Revised Standard Version (RSV), a complete revision of the American Standard Version (1901) in the tradition of the King James Bible, was undertaken by thirty scholars in 1937. It was completed in 1952. It was made available in American and English editions. It sought to present as accurate a translation as possible while upholding standards of English diction appropriate to public and private worship.

NEW REVISED STANDARD VERSION

The New Revised Standard Version (NRSV) was published in 1990 and is a far-reaching revision of the RSV. It has done away with "thee" and "thou" and "art" (for "are") and "dost" (for "do"). It has tried, where possible, to use language which does not exclude women. Nevertheless the NRSV tries to remain as close to the originals as possible while maintaining the high literary standards of the RSV.

JERUSALEM BIBLE

The Jerusalem Bible (JB) is the work of Roman Catholic scholars, mostly British. It is based on a careful examination of the Hebrew and Greek originals but it follows the French *Bible de Jerusalem*. It attempts to present poetic parts of the originals in a suitable modern poetic idiom. Above all, it strives for clarity of expression, often, it must be said at the expense of the original meaning. It is the translation most frequently used in public worship in Roman Catholic churches of the English-speaking world.

NEW JERUSALEM BIBLE

The New Jerusalem Bible (NJB) is a revision of the JB and was published in 1985. It seeks to be more faithful than the JB to the original Hebrew and Greek and is more consistent in its translation of words. It tries to maintain the high poetic quality of its predecessor and it uses inclusive language whenever possible.

NEW ENGLISH BIBLE

The New English Bible (NEB) broke away from the influence of the KJB (AV) and sought "to say in our own native idiom what we believed the author to be saying in his". Scholars representing nearly all the major churches in Great Britain and Ireland managed to produce a translation which is lucid, fresh and natural, if, on occasion, somewhat basic. It is a Bible in plain rather than ornate English.

REVISED ENGLISH BIBLE

The Revised English Bible (REB) appeared in 1989 as a complete and thorough revision of the NEB. It shuns "thou" and "thee" and half-heartedly attempts to use inclusive language. Its efforts to provide an even fresher and more vivid translation that its predecessor are not always successful.

NEW AMERICAN BIBLE

The New American Bible (NAB) is the first English Bible to be translated from the original Hebrew and Greek texts by American Catholic scholars. It has been partly updated by revision in 1987. It attempts to render the original texts as closely as possible while intent on conveying the meaning as clearly as possible. It is surprisingly weak in its efforts to embrace inclusive language and it is conservative in its use of modern English idioms. The English of the NAB is, of course, American.

GOOD NEWS BIBLE

The Good News Bible (GNB), sometimes called Today's English Version (TEV) was completed in 1976. The GNB attempts to provide a translation easily accessible to all who read English, whether as a first or second language, while aiming to reproduce the meaning of the original texts as closely as possible. Every effort has been made to use language that is clear, simple and unambiguous. A feature of the GNB is the line drawings by the Swiss artist, Annie Vallotton. The GNB is Britain's most popular Bible. Its aim to use the language of ordinary people occasionally leads to over-simplification of the original texts.

NEW INTERNATIONAL VERSION

The New International Version (NIV) was produced in 1978 by an international team of scholars who sought to avoid sectarian bias in their work. Based on the best available manuscripts, it seeks faithfulness to the originals and clarity of style. It aims, therefore, to be suitable for public reading and private study. Its advertisers claim it to be the most trustworthy of all modern translations, a claim not all would concede.

NEW KING JAMES BIBLE

The New King James Bible (NKJB) or Revised Authorised Version (RAV), published in 1982, is an attempt to preserve the historic dignity of the original KJB of 1611 but to update all that is no longer easily understood. It is the Bible most used by conservative Protestants in the United States (when not using the KJB). It has much of the glory of the old King James and all of its defects.

RHEIMS-DOUAI BIBLE

The Rheims-Douai Bible has nurtured Roman Catholics throughout the English-speaking world for the past few centuries. It bears all the scars of its history. It was a fine translation when completed in 1610. It suffered then what it suffers now. Like all translations of its time, it was made when scholars did not have available to them the vast amount of manuscripts in Hebrew and Greek now available. Consequently, like Tyndale and the King James, it cannot be depended upon to provide an accurate translation of what the original authors wrote. It is not now widely available and it is time to lay an old servant to rest.

THE CHRISTIAN COMMUNITY BIBLE

The Christian Community Bible is the work of Roman Catholic Missionary scholars with direct experience of the human condition from the centre to the fringes of human existence, from Europe to South America to Asia; experiences of the human condition in the rich city centres, impoverished villages and destitute favelas and slums that surround both. The translation is based on the Hebrew and Greek texts and has taken utmost care to respect the original scope of the "Word" which is "a gift from God to humanity".

The extensive introductions and notes explain the theological, spiritual, sacramental and social life of the Christian Community in the light of the Scriptures thus making both intelligible and accessible to all the members of the community. In a number countries the CCB has become the official translation of the local Church and often a place also in the liturgical use and group study.

And finally ...

Almost all publishers of modern Bibles provide a great range of editions. One may purchase a Bible in paperback without any notes or aids of any kind. One may buy a large hardback edition with splendid maps, introductory notes to each section and book and helpful footnotes to guide the reader through the text. Some publish large print editions, helpful to those with impaired eyesight. Some highlight the words of Jesus in red print. Indeed, at no time in history have English-speaking people had such a variety of excellent translations of the ancient scriptures of Jews and Christians. To benefit from this happy state of affairs, the first-time buyer would do well to purchase a Bible with all the aids that modern scholarship and modern publishers can provide. This may cost at little more than one anticipated but buying a Bible is like buying anything else: you get what you pay for.

By the same author

MARK MY WORDS

It is in the firm belief that an understanding of the Gospels, and, in this case, of the Gospel according to Mark, that is rooted in good scholarship, in pastoral concern and in not a little passion for the figure of Jesus of Nazareth, that *Mark My Words* is offered to its readers. By a sensitive reading of his words, the author seeks, in the plainest of language, to make Mark alive, in his historical setting and in his contemporary relevance.

This book will greatly benefit those who must preach Mark's compelling story, those who must teach in parish or school so that hearts burn within when the Scriptures are disclosed. It will enrich all who seek to know, in the words of Francis of Assisi, God's "most holy written words" and the one who came from God "to receive the flesh of humanity."

ISBN 085439 472 9   316 pages

ST PAULS

THE PSALMS

Translated by Joseph Rhymer
Introductions by Angelo Lancellotti

.

To make the psalms accessible to our contemporaries, to help them understand these as expressive of their needs and aspirations, is an important and not easy task. This accurate and delightful "new" translation of the psalms offers a new perspective on their meaning for the individual and the community from the biblical times to the present.

There is an exhaustive introduction to the entire Psalter by an outstanding biblical scholar which is followed by a shorter topical introduction to each of the psalms. In Professor Lancellotti's comprehensive introduction to this modern version of the psalms, the clergy, theologians and students of scripture and theology, catechists and liturgists, and the laity who have made the psalms their daily prayer have a knowledgeable and reliable guide.

ISBN 085439 474 5   435 pages

ST PAULS